M[
Review

Vol. 2 No. 4 Spring 2012

Black-lava Malpaís/badlands in western New Mexico

"The Badlands are everywhere"

Malpaís Review

po box 339

Placitas, NM 87043

The Meaning of *Malpaís*

The Spanish word "malpaís" (badlands) is a term that can have wide and narrow meaning. Badlands can be inside and outside, artistic, psychological, geographical, political and historical. The literal black-lava badlands in New Mexico are most prominent in the western part of the state where the Malpaís National Monument is located. The famous badlands of South Dakota, which are not volcanic, and others, take different forms but have common meaning.

There are many applications of the word "malpaís." Politically, the nation has gone through a long period of badlands in the last 25 years or so, which has greatly eroded what little remains of American democracy. Artists go through periodic "badlands" of blank page or blank canvas, though these are not permanent. But whatever the literal or metaphorical nature of the term, the badlands are everywhere.

The texts in this publication, we hope, will help to discover personal and collective badlands, so they can be dealt with and maybe offer some guidance or serve as some sort of sustenance in crossing the badlands, wherever they are located and whatever meaning they have for our readers.

Malpaís **Review** is available thru Amazon.com and these bookstores: Alamosa Books, Page One, and Acequia Booksellers in Albuquerque, NM; Range Cafe Store, Bernalillo, NM; Rollin'R Gallery in Placitas, NM; Op Cit Bookstore in Santa Fe, NM (930C Baca Street), and Beyond Baroque in Los Angeles, CA.

Subscriptions:
> $42 for one year (4 issues) postage paid
> $55 to institutions for one year (" ") " "

Single copies by mail:
> $12 + $3.50 shipping and handling
> Make checks payable to Gary Brower, and mail to *Malpaís* Review, po box 339, Placitas, NM 87043

For Contributor Biographies, please see last pages of this issue.
For Submission Guidelines, please see last pages of this issue.
For Photo, Art and Poem Credits, see last pages of this issue.

ISSN 2153-4918
Malpaisreview.com

Malpaís Review

Vol. 2 No. 4 Spring 2012

Editorial staff:
  Editor: Gary L. Brower
  Associate Editor: Dale Harris
  Art Editor: Marilyn Stablein
  Guest Editor: Hakim Bellamy
  Southern California correspondent:
      Suzanne Lummis
  Staff Photographer: J. M. Gay, Jr
  Graphic Designer and Assistant Editor:
      Esther Feske
  Website: Kenneth P. Gurney
Advisory board:
  Renny Golden
  E. A. "Tony" Mares
  Simon Ortiz
  Charles Potts
  Margaret Randall
Malpaís Review name and slogan: Todd Moore

Just published: **Leaving Cairo, As If It Were A Dream** by Gary L. Brower (poems), James M. Gay, Jr. (photos) and John Bullock (CD & music), published by *Malpaís* Editions and available from Malpais Review, P.O. Box 339, Placitas, NM 87043 ($20).

On the covers: "Time on My Hands" and "Time Travel" collages are by Marilyn Stablein, our art editor.
Interior art (pages 65, 185, 214, 227) are photos of assemblage sculptures, each painted a uniform color, by William Georgenes. All are untitled.

Contents

Editor's Note

There has been a lot going on locally, nationally, and internationally in the world of poetry, as usual, but you don't find it all in one place, so I try to bring together what I can in each Editor's Note to attempt to give some perspective to it all. Locally, one of the biggest events for some time was the *Librotraficante* caravan and readings; that story is a feature in this issue.

If you think poetry doesn't cause controversy, then look at the explosion caused by one poem by German Nobel Prize winner (1999) Gunter Grass, published in the *Suddeutsch Zeitung,* and certain other European newspapers, on April 4, 2012. Although known more for his prose, like the great "Danziger Trilogy" of novels (**The Tin Drum, Cat and Mouse, Dog Years**), Grass has also published a number of poetry books over the years.

Grass (now 85) has had a controversial literary (and non-literary) life: a supporter of the political Left after World War II, he encouraged Germany to deal with its Nazi past. Then, after 60 years of silence, he revealed in his memoir that he had been drafted at age 17 into the Waffen SS at the end of that war. Given his outspoken urgings for Germany and Germans to "come clean," this seemed like hypocrisy on his part, and it caused an uproar everywhere. And now it is being brought up to attack him by those who don't like this political poem, "What must be said." Even supporters have said it isn't very good, poetically in German or otherwise. It is an attack on Israeli Prime Minister Benjamin Netanyahu's warlike threats against Iran. But the immediate cause was the decision of the current German Government to sell submarines to Israel that have the capacity to launch nuclear missiles. Grass saw this as Germans aiding a possible nuclear campaign that could cause a worldwide catastrophe. Right-wingers have tried to claim Grass is anti-Semitic and anti-Israel for daring to criticize the Netanyahu government, as if the current Prime Minister were synonymous with the nation-state itself. This is, of course, like saying you couldn't criticize the Bush regime when they were ruining the U.S. because it would mean you were criticizing the U.S. itself. As a result, Israel has declared that Grass is barred from entering (although he has traveled there in the past). Obviously the earlier Labor (Socialist) Party founding governments of Israel are very different from the Right-Wing governments of recent years.

Newspapers all over the world made editorial statements about this controversy. Here is a comment from the left-leaning German paper *Die Tageszeitung*: "The problem is not that Grass has sharply criticized the Israeli Government for their policies on Iran. Such criticism is common and all too justified. But Grass uses the publication of his poem for something altogether different: He excuses his long silence with the fear of being blasted as an anti-Semite." And from Charles Hawley in the left-leaning *Berliner Zeitung*: "The nuclear power Israel, Grass writes, is a danger to the fragile global peace. It is certainly a defensible thesis. Benjamin Netanyahu seems uninterested in compromise, not with the Palestinians, and not with the Iranians. On the other side, Grass sees only a loudmouth (Mahmoud Achmadinejad) who likely doesn't even possess atomic weapons." Grass himself once said that lyric is the form of writing that is the most explicit and clear, which may be why he said all of this in poetry. But, the writer continues, Grass is "blind in one eye," meaning he is harder on Netanyahu than on Achmadinejad. In any case, you, the reader can decide what you think of the poem, here it is:

What must be said
by Gunter Grass

Why do I stay silent, conceal for too long
what clearly is and has been
practiced in war games, at the end of which we as
       survivors
are at best footnotes.

It is the alleged right to first strike
that could annihilate the Iranian people—
enslaved by a loudmouth
and guided to organized jubilation—
because in their territory,
it is suspected, a bomb is being built.

8

Yet why do I forbid myself
to name that other country
in which, for years, even if secretly,
there has been a growing nuclear potential at hand
but beyond control, because no inspection is available?

The universal concealment of these facts,
to which my silence subordinated itself,
I sense as incriminating lies
and force—the punishment is promised
as soon as it is ignored;
the verdict of "anti-Semitism" is familiar.

Now, though, because in my country
which from time to time has sought and confronted
its very own crime
that is without compare
in turn on a purely commercial basis, if also
with nimble lips calling it a reparation, declares
a further U-boat should be delivered to Israel,
whose specialty consists of guiding all-destroying
              warheads to where the existence
of a single atomic bomb is unproven,
but as a fear wishes to be conclusive,
I say what must be said.

Why though have I stayed silent until now?
Because I thought my origin,
afflicted by a stain never to be expunged
kept the state of Israel, to which I am bound,
from accepting this fact as pronounced truth.

Why do I say only now,
aged and with my last ink,
that the nuclear power of Israel endangers
the already fragile world peace?
Because it must be said
what even tomorrow may be too late to say:
also because we—as Germans burdened enough—
could be the suppliers to a crime

that is foreseeable, wherefore our complicity
could not be redeemed through any of the usual excuses.

And granted: I am silent no longer
because I am tired of the hypocrisy
of the West; in addition to which it is to be hoped
that this will free many from silence,
that they may prompt the perpetrator of the recognized
       danger
to renounce violence and
likewise insist
that an unhindered and permanent control
of the Israeli nuclear potential
and the Iranian nuclear sites
be authorized through an international agency
by the governments of both countries.

Only this way are all, the Israelis and Palestinians,
even more, all people, that in this
region occupied by mania
live cheek by jowl among enemies,
and also us, to be helped.

(Translation by Heather Horn; from an online site).

***

In this issue, we honor three poets who have recently passed
away and whose work was excellent: Harvena Richter of
Albuquerque, who was not well known in recent years; the very
famous Adrienne Rich, one of the best poets in the nation; and
Gene Frumkin (1928–2007). They will be missed, and we trust
you will appreciate our tributes to them.

Also, shortly before publication of this issue, we heard of the
death of poet Reed Whittemore (1919-2012), another writer not
well known today. He lived in Washington, D.C. for many years
after retiring as Professor Emeritus from the University of
Maryland (1968-84). He published some dozen books of poetry
and a biography, *William Carlos Williams: Poet from Jersey* (1975),
which was well considered by critics. Whittemore served twice

as Poet Laureate of the U.S. (it was called "Poetry Consultant to the Library of Congress" at that time) in 1964 and 1984 (this time filling in for the ailing Robert Fitzgerald). He was also Poet Laureate of Maryland. While a student at Yale, Whittemore founded a literary journal, *Furioso*, once called the best of the little magazines, in which he published the likes of William Carlos Williams, Ezra Pound, e.e. cummings, Marianne Moore and Wallace Stevens. After serving in WWII, he taught at Carleton College in Minnesota where he revived the magazine as the *Carleton Miscellany*. He was eventually the literary editor of *The New Republic* and remained a supporter of little magazines throughout his life. Some of his books of poetry are: **Heroes & Heroines** (1946), **The Self-Made Man** (1959), **The Feel of Rock: Poems of Three Decades** (1982), and **The Mother's Breast & the Father's House**, a finalist for the National Book Award. In 2007, he published a memoir, **Against the Grain**, with an introduction by Garrison Keillor.

And speaking of Poets Laureate, congratulations to Hakim Bellamy for being named the first Albuquerque Poet Laureate; see picture & caption at the beginning of our feature on African-American poets, which Hakim edited. I thank Hakim for bringing together an excellent anthology, joining local poets with such nationally known quality poets as Sonia Sánchez and E. Ethelbert Miller.

I also want to thank and congratulate those who have helped bring the large segments about Álvaro Cardona-Hine and Gene Frumkin into *Malpaís Review*. These features are connected in many ways: they were good friends going back to their days in Los Angeles, good poets, and "good people" as the phrase goes. They were part of that seminal group of poets around the great Tom McGrath, years ago. John Tritica, who wrote the essay on Gene Frumkin's work and assisted in many other ways, is thanked profusely. Likewise, the assistance provided by David Abel is greatly appreciated; he has graciously provided unpublished poems of Gene's (the book will be issued soon). This set of poems link poetry to the visual arts through Gene's focus on works that spoke to him. As someone who likes to see the arts linked in this way, I found these poems to be especially appealing. Of course, I am extremely grateful to George Kalamaras for his incredible interview with Álvaro Cardona-Hine, one of the best I've seen with any poet. The interview burrows into the Past, the Present, and how the biography is related to the artist's work. We know that the author's biography is not the same as his work, for we hope those works will outlive the artist. But this interview helps us see what formed both art and artist. And it shows the direct relation between two excellent poets who became New Mexicans. We miss Gene but we are delighted to still have Álvaro with us. These two features had to be published together. Another angle is that Holly Prado, one of Los Angeles' most well known poets, had Álvaro as a mentor many years ago, which is why her poems connect the two segments.

I thank our art director, Marilyn Stablein, for use of her collages on the covers, a departure from past covers. I think it gives us a new look and I hope our readers will find them appealing. Thanks also to William Georgenes for his complex sculptures, which are made of toys, household items, tubing and mysterious objects, all sprayed to one color; we like their Surreal quality.

I want to note that the U.S. Postal Service issued a set of stamps April 21, honoring poets Sylvia Plath, William Carlos Williams, Elizabeth Bishop, Denise Levertov, e.e. cummings, Theodore Roethke, Gwendolyn Brooks, Wallace Stevens, Joseph Brodsky, and Robert Hayden.

And finally, I want to recommend a non-poetry book, **Lies My Teacher Told Me** by James W. Loewen (NY, Simon & Schuster, 2007 edition), which contrasts American history with what is in school textbooks, an enlightening work. —GLB

Poetry Never Stood a Chance of Standing Outside History

Farewell to Adrienne Rich (1929-2012)

by Margaret Randall

Adrienne Rich at Ghost Ranch, New Mexico, 1990s

There are voices that change a language forever. César Vallejo did this to Spanish. Adrienne Rich did it for English. Great poets take the raw materials—events, tragedy, character and survival—of a time and place, and inject the pulsing brilliance of their singular voices, giving us words to help us live. Such was Rich's offering. Her legacy will feed us as long as we have memory. Margalit Fox, in her New York Times obituary, speaks of work "distinguished by an unswerving progressive vision and a dazzling, empathic ferocity."[1] I would add that the poet was a deeply personal yet eloquently monumental voice in a time when women continue to have to struggle to make ourselves heard.

The trajectory of Rich's life in poetry is well known: her early education in the classics she found on the shelves of

---

[1] "Adrienne Rich, Feminist Poet, Dies at 82," *New York Times*, March 28, 2012.

her father's library (all men, she would later say); W. H. Auden choosing her first collection of poems, **A Change of World**, as the winner of the prestigious Yale Younger Poets series in 1950; the groundbreaking **Snapshots of a Daughter-in-Law** published the same year as Betty Friedan's **The Feminine Mystique** (1963); and subsequent collections up until the very end of her life, each further enriching a body of work that may well be considered the literary conscience of several generations.

Her prose was no less important. Essays such as "Of Woman Born (1976), "On Lies, Secrets, and Silence (1979), "Blood, Bread, and Poetry" (1986), and "Compulsory Heterosexuality and Lesbian Existence" (1981) broke age-old barriers and helped shape identities in a time of turmoil, change, and an obscenely twisted public discourse. In both her poetry and prose, Rich did nothing less than explain us to ourselves.

I met Adrienne Rich in Nicaragua in 1983. Invited by the Sandinistas, she came to an international gathering of artists and intellectuals. The U.S.-backed Contra war was raging, and among the hundreds in attendance she was one of only a handful who signed up to make the difficult trip to the war zone. Our small caravan progressed slowly, stopping frequently so the young men and women responsible for our safety could check the area for possible ambushes. It wasn't an easy trip, but Rich—already severely crippled by the rheumatoid arthritis that eventually took her life—was an example of patience, calm and enthusiasm.

Neither of us knew that only a few years later I would return to the United States and be ordered deported because of opinions expressed in some of my books. Rich, always a staunch defender of freedom of expression, was an expert witness at my 1986 trial in El Paso, Texas. As always, she was brilliant. But the true measure of her generosity and character came through in the many acts of solidarity she dispensed throughout that long week.

Rich was consistent in the defense of her values, even when it meant refusing important honors most writers would accept no matter how they might have to justify it to themselves

Audre Lorde, Meridel LeSueur, and Adrienne Rich, 1980

and others. In 1974, rather than receive the National Book Award for Poetry for herself alone, she appeared onstage with two of that year's finalists, Audre Lorde and Alice Walker.[2] They accepted the distinction on behalf of all women. In 1997, Rich declined the National Medal of Arts, the highest award our government bestows upon artists. She expressed her dismay at being one of a few token artists honored while "the people at large [endure the] increasingly brutal impact of racial and economic injustice." Among the numerous honors she did accept, were a MacArthur Foundation "genius" grant in 1994, a National Book Award for poetry in 1974, the Bollingen Prize for Poetry, and the Ruth Lilly Poetry Prize.

Adrienne Rich spoke truth to power in her work and in the many large and small acts people who came in contact with her remember. Midwest poet Lyle Daggett tells the following story: "On September 12, 2001, Adrienne Rich was scheduled to read her poems on the University of Minnesota campus. After the World Trade Center was destroyed the day before and all flights were grounded, the University shut down classes for the day on the 12th – similar things were happening all over the United States. I called the university English department and reached a recording saying that the department office was closed for the day, and that classes were cancelled; then the recording

-----

[2] Rich shared the award that year with Allen Ginsberg..

15

said that Rich's reading would go on that evening as scheduled. After work I headed for the campus. It was in a large modern theater building on the West Bank side of the campus, on the high cliffs above the Mississippi river. There was no admission charge. The large room was packed. The air in the theater was charged more highly than any place I've ever been. A professor from the English department introduced her, and explained that Rich had been in Kansas City on the 11th, and when flights were grounded she hired a driver and they drove for 13 hours through the night to Minneapolis so she could do the reading here. The professor finished her introduction and Adrienne Rich came out and read. It was one of the truly great poetry readings I've been to in my life. I can't think of a better place to have been that evening."

I find no greater or more appropriate way to honor the poet than with her own words. And so I will end this brief tribute with a fragment of her astonishing "North American Time," as relevant now as when she wrote it in the mid 1980s:

> II
> Everything we write
> will be used against us
> or against those we love.
> These are the terms,
> take them or leave them.
>
> Poetry never stood a chance
> of standing outside history.
> One line typed twenty years ago
> can be blazed on a wall in spraypaint
> to glorify art as detachment
> or torture of those we
> did not love but also
> did not want to kill
>
> We move   but our words stand
> become responsible
> for more than we intended . . .

16

Andrea J. Serrano
An Open Letter to Governor Martínez*

For New Mexico's First Latina Governor

Dear Susana
I want to understand you
sew you to myself
with the common thread
I thought existed between us
I want to weave you into the fabric of my being
I want to admire you

I want to laugh with you
reminisce with you
I want us to drink too much wine
sing *Paloma Negra*
and cry together

What were you like as a little girl?
Did you run carefree in fields of flowers?
I imagine you
nestled safely in your father's arms
as you crossed the El Paso/Juarez border
maybe to visit family
that stayed behind
when your grandparents crossed the border
or just to go shopping
I see your tiny brown fist
clutching a *paleta*
savoring the sweetness of Mexico on your tongue

When did you stop crossing?
When did you develop a bitter taste in your mouth
for people who, at one time, were just your neighbors?

We are not so different
you and I
we are women

we are ambitious
smart
powerful
and Brown
we advocate for children and women
victims of abuse
did you ask them for papers before you helped them?
Would you now?

What was it like
to trade your people for power
your people for position
did you even allow yourself to think about it?

It would be wonderful to be proud of you
to hold you up
celebrate you
I wish I could say
"*mira,* she's one of us"
but you feel so far away
so un-like a sister
let me say it again

you feel so far away
so un-like a sister
you feel foreign
you are a stranger

I am afraid of you
of what you will do to hold on to the power
that was handed to you
gifted by the people who see you as a joke
a farce
you are being used to divide and conquer
Governor in brown face
I'm afraid of what desperation will make you do next

I want to understand you
but I don't
I can't
I wouldn't
not to my own
not to anybody

Do you get lonely?
Do you get tired?
Do you wish to seek comfort in your people
only to find
we aren't there.

---

*New Mexico Governor Susana Martínez, a conservative Republican, was elected in 2010, the first woman to govern the state and the first latina to be elected to the governorship in any state. She has also sponsored anti-immigrant legislation, even though many years ago her family crossed from Mexico into El Paso, TX, where she grew up.

Cathy Arellano
Gentrification Is When

my land has more value
when you own it

you're invited to the neighborhood association
i've never seen the welcome mat

you move to my neighborhood for diversity
don't do a damn thing to diversify your own hometown

you stroll carefree through my neighborhood
i'm pulled over for "driving while brown" through yours

you buy your starter house
evict me from my dream home

you move in and the corner grocery store
stops stocking my nana's #1 ingredient: affordable

bike lanes go up where there always were bikes
just brown riders

the city sweeps the streets and installs lights at Dolores Park for
          you
builds a new jail at 17th and Valencia for me

you drink straight from the bottle or can and light up without
          worry in the park
i'm arrested while walking by for "fitting the description"

hundreds of you never make a mob no matter how noisy you are
two of me is a gang

you think this poem is a joke
i don't care what you think
but i have to

Cathy Arellano
Mission Walls

US OUT OF EL SALVADOR
on Carl's Bakery
Esther says,
We had maids and a big house
before the communists came.
She lives in the projects on Harrison.
I don't believe her
but I'm still her friend

US OUT OF NICARAGUA
on Mission High School
Uncle Mickey says he's going to a meeting
with his Comité.
The rest of the adults in our house
speak Democrat
not Republican
not Sandinista.
Uncle marches with his group.
Later, he drafts me and Fran
to volunteer at the Gay Parade.
I'm 15 and terrified.

FMLN
on Everett Middle School

FSLN
in Dearborn alley

Yankee Go Home
everywhere.

It was years before I knew
I was a Yankee
or a Revolutionary.

Cathy Arellano
Taos Summer of Love

summer of love flags beckon
rainbow tie dye children of all ages
wander the plaza
just as lost as first explorers

black work boots kick dirt with each step
from truck bed to flower bed
perpetual motion
in 7,000 mile high heat

in faces of brown men in green coveralls
i recognize cousins and uncles
from summer of love city
1,000 miles away

one notices my pen and paper
stops and asks,
are you with a class?

yes

are you from here?

no
my turn: are you?

yes, my family's been here since…
we're Spanish
are you Spanish?

in the early 1980s
back home on the left coast
summer-loving chicanos jammed sidewalks for
the mission's 1st International Cruise Night

cars hopped higher than yardsticks at 24th
bombs crawled down mission street
brentan wood oogum boogumed

with his bad self
from every open window

josie g.,
whose name you could find on any wall in the mission
in front of, behind, beneath, or on top of my sister's,
lisa a.
and always with a big fat
Con/Safos
told us of her daddy's homeland:
24th and Mission is cool
san jo's got it going on with Story and King
and there ain't nothing wrong with East Los
but Española, New Mexico
that's The Lowrider Capital of the WORLD!

The world?

The world!

Fer realz?

she maddogged us.
we raised our underage hands
with overage drinks
to those chicanos
who gave lowriding
a capital!

after my first and last party
with my sister and her homegirls
cops killed mission street cruising
no left turns 9 pm to 4 am
you got a broken tail light
expired registration
pull over

our dreams
if we had any
crashed into jail and drugs,
we got pregnant

we dropped out

i grabbed my journal and ran
didn't look back
til i was in a history class
on a college campus

where i learned i was aztec,
azteca, mexica royalty
forgot that grandpa
told my cousins and me
We're *Yaqui*
forgot that my *Rarámuri*[1] great-grandmother
was stolen from the river
when she was 12

i learned about old spain, new spain,
la raza cósmica[2]
and those chicanos
who think they're spanish
trace bloodlines east across ocean
not south across border

are you spanish?

ten years back in sf
san francisco not santa fe
art commission planned
soldier statue to grace entrance
of city's oldest church

mission dolores
where my family of crooked catholics
makes first communions
confirmations
marries
says good-bye

today, that first church,
and the new basilica,
and mission high

and dolores park
cover 5,000 unmarked graves
of natives begged borrowed and stolen

are you spanish?

300 years after Popé [3]
led *pueblos* and *genízaros*[4] (heneeeezaros)
in the first american revolution
and they paid for their rebellion
at the end of ropes in this plaza

are you spanish?

in this unfamiliar land
familiar eyes search mine
i know his question is
are you *raza*?
i tell my brother
sí

---

[1] *Rarámuri*=Tarahumara tribe of NW Mexico
[2] *La raza cosmica*=The book & concept by Mexican writer Jose
Vasconcelos, which predicted a future "race" in the Americas that is a
mixture of all races in the region, a positive combination that will lead
to a better world.
[3] Popé=leader of the Pueblo Revolt of 1680 which threw the Spanish out
of New Mexico for 12 years
[4] *pueblos* and *genízaros*=Native Americans and mixed indo-hispanic
people, especially in New Mexico

James McGrath
Directions For Walking In Mud

Whatever you leave behind will be gone
     in the Spring.

Tie your shoes with a double knot.

Once you enter the mud field, look back
     to see the pattern your shoes leave
     for your shadow to follow.

Never leave your shadow alone
     in the liquid wilderness.

Each step you take has its own name.

Listen as your feet whisper the same myth
     over and over as if in alphabetical order.

Winter mud is for remembering how the earth
     blooms, why the waters of snow-melt
     are colorless like the center of a stars eye
     watching who comes to your door.

Should you wish to count the tracks
     of small birds, you must first name them,
     give them their power. This is how
     you learn their songs.

Should you wish to return to where you began
     before nightfall, fill your footsteps
     with memories of when you were young
     and could count to ten

This is where your path began by walking alone.
     This is when you made mud-pies for the secret
     companion you now reach out to hold their hand
     to your heart.

This is when Spring begins all over again.

James McGrath
Weaving On A Spring Morning

I watch the rise and fall of his ribs,
      listen to his breathing, how he weaves
      earth sounds and bird songs into
      his morning prayers.

My Mother said, "Your father is a lonely man.
      He sings with birds that lose their way,
      carves stones that praise wounded dogs
      and animals crushed on back roads "

I sit very still, ears open, eyes in a squint
      when I watch my morning Father.

He knows I am there. He touches my head
      when the sun rises. He leaves feathers
      on my pillow in the Spring when birds
      build their nests in the willows
      by the river.

This is how my Father and I s p e a k.

Linda Whittenberg
'Til There Was You

Cassandra Wilson Concert, 2008

Music like a sluggish, peeved, river—
mosquitoes swarm the muddy surface,
catfish nose for bottom scraps,
steam and sadness hover.
Not sad like crying in your drink,
more like a fading bruise, blue, lavender,
even green. Despair bursting
into early blossoms, promise of peach.

'Til there was you.
Piano man, Converse high-tops pumping.
Guitar player, bows in adoration over strings, his lovely face
color of almonds—
Birds, but I couldn't see them winging.
Drum, heat of Congo, sweaty pate,
smooth mahogany, dew on verdant leaves.
Bass, limber-jack loose,
long fingers like God, plucking that first rhythm,
twanging, pointing, plucking
heart strings of the world.

Music, I never heard it singing.
Wang, wang of bent chords
'Til there was you.
Pulse thrums to something remembered. Feet tap and twitch,
skin tingles in answer to electric, rhythmic frenzy.
Bodies rock back and forth in compulsive response
to primal call.

Cassandra's voice, smooth as sap oozing from wounded
      sycamore,
timbre sweet as honey from lush clover,
I never heard them singing.
Golden sacrifice of bees
on a hot Mississippi day
with rain clouds gathering,
river rising.

Hakim Bellamy:
Albuquerque's First Poet Laureate

On Saturday, April 14, 2012, Albuquerque Mayor Richard Berry invested Hakim Bellamy as the first-ever Poet Laureate of the city. New Mexico's capital city, Santa Fe, had done this earlier and is now looking for its fourth Poet Laureate. The first was Arthur Sze, the second Valerie Martínez, and the current occupant of the position is Joan Logghe, who has a few weeks left in her tenure. As in Albuquerque, this is a two-year appointment. Joan and Valerie spoke at the Saturday event, and read poems, along with New Mexico's Statehood Centennial Poet Levi Romero. Various members of the original committee to create, organize, and lobby for the position were in attendance, as well as the final committee which chose the candidate, who was not revealed until the Mayor mentioned his name. The event was held in the auditorium of the Main Library in downtown Albuquerque.

Sponsors of the Poet Laureate program, which is under the fiscal umbrella of the Escuela del Sol Montessori/Harwood Art Center (a 501c3 organization), include: McCune Charitable Foundation, ABC Libraries, Friends of the Public Library, Kenneth Gurney/Adobe Walls Anthology & Poetry Venue, Billy Brown & the Fixed & Free Poetry Venue, Janet Brennan, ABQ Hiking & Outdoor Meetup, Gayle Lauradunn, Norty & Summer Kalishman, and the ABQ Chapter of the New Mexico State Poetry Society. Donations may be sent to: APLP, c/o Susan McAllister, 3333 Purdue NE, ABQ, NM 87106. Make checks out to Escuela del Sol, marked APLP in the memo. Contact for the organizing committee or the Poet Laureate: contact@abqpoetlaureate.org. Website: www.abqpoetlaureate.org.   —GLB

Soul Food For The Hungry

by Hakim Bellamy

I speak to the black experience, but I am always talking about the human condition — about what we can endure, dream, fail at, and still survive.
— Dr. Maya Angelou

Black poetry is like slam poetry. It is poetry so titled, because of who performs it, and where it is performed. If, in fact, a poem is delivered at a poetry slam by a poet (considered a "slam" poet by default of where they deliver their poem) is a slam poem, what happens when that poem is published first? If a poem is published before it is read at a poetry slam is it categorically a page poem or a slam poem? In contrast, it is extremely difficult for me to write a poem before being Black. So will my poetry always be Black?

I share this mental exercise in full appreciation of the opportunity extended me by Gary Brower to curate a mini-anthology of African American poetry for the *Malpais* **Review**. This opportunity serves to illuminate the importance of including *and* separating such poetry in this day and age. By singling out and spotlighting the unique and significant contribution of Black poetry to American language, literature, and life, we simultaneously include it, integrate into our psyche, soul, and history.

Made black and white on the page, poetry can exist devoid of artistic performance. Whether "stage" poet or "page" poet, the poem starts with the writing process, before we later ascribe a style, genre or aesthetic to it. Long before we choose to perform it at a lecture, in a coffee shop, a bar, a library, at a rally, or on a street corner, we are piecing together the "what" of the poem. The "what" of the poem, happens long before the "where" and "when" of the poem. The "what" happens before the "how" of the poem as well, whether we are recalling how to write a sestina, sonnet, prose or "slam" poem.

However, the "who" of the poem happens pre-writing. The "who" of the poem happens before the ability to write, type or hold a pencil. It happens pre- fine motor skills, pre-speech and pre-birth. It is pre-literate and pre-literature. Who we are is beyond our individual lives. The context that creates our lived reality as men, women, Black, indigenous, young and old is molding and has been molding for generations.

Generally, as Black poets, we do not fight being Black, but we often fight to be more than *just* "Black poets" in a society that seems hellbent on fighting our fight. However, the "who" that America is actually fighting is itself. There is an institutional desire to separate past from present and trauma from triumph. The desire to separate the Black experience in America that remembers and reminds from the black spots on the American legacy that would rather be forgotten.

We cannot forget who we are. The "who" is about identity. The identities that we perform on a daily basis are connected to and defined by history. Both our personal and collective histories inform how others perceive and how we perform our identity as men, women, people of means, people of none, and people of color. As individuals, we perpetually make choices as to whether we perform our current identity in accordance with or in opposition to our personal histories, our collective history, and people's perception of who we are. However, the one thing we cannot choose is to perform our identities absent of our history.

Black poetry emerges as the thorn out of the side of the rosy history and tradition that America fantasizes about and fabricates. It is the piece of American history and literature that must be acknowledged, like an addiction. Like an alcoholic, America must first admit to a history of abuse before it can recover, repair, and rectify. Like an alcoholic, America is in denial. We are suffering from a history of decisions we may or may not have made. A history of decisions sadly embedded in our DNA. However, like an alcoholic we are more than the parts of our history we would like to forget; and we can even be better than those parts of our history, if we reckon with it instead of run.

Black poetry belongs to all of us and though not everyone can write "Black" poetry, everyone can benefit from it. Just like we all can't be doctors or priests, but we all need healing at one time or another. This collection of African American poetry can be considered soul food for the hungry. From Philadelphia Poet Laureate and Black Arts Movement icon Sonia Sánchez's hunger for justice in "14 haiku *(for Emmet Louis Till)*" to Jabari Asad's (the youngest poet anthologized here) hunger for childhood, I contend that we can and should feed our past to our future in order to make it stronger. Hunger is a human condition that knows no color. Just like good poetry, both are felt in the gut. And though I am unsure if there is such a thing as "good" hunger, there is the requisite ongoing debate over what constitutes "good" and "bad" poetry – a debate that is both healthy and subjective. However, what *good* poetry makes us feel is more universal and far less subjective than people's poetic preferences. I argue that *good* poetry is made no different by how, when, or where one shares it. It is a feeling, an experience, a fact. It is a need. A need that might be met or unmet, but a need that will certainly never go unacknowledged. Welcome to a poetic interpretation of the Black experience in America.

Sonia Sánchez
10 haiku

(for Max Roach)

1.
Nothing ends
every blade of grass
remembering your sound

2.
your sounds exploding
in the universe return
to earth in prayer

3.
as you drummed
your hands kept
reaching for God

4.
the morning sky
so lovely imitates
your laughter

5.
you came warrior
clear your music
kissing our spines

6.
feet tapping
singing, impeach
our blood

7.
you came drumming
sweet life on
sails of flesh

8.
your fast beat
riding the air settles
in our bones

9.
your drums
soloing our breaths into
the beat . . . unbeat

10.
your hands
shimmering on the
legs of rain.

Jasmine Cuffee

Terminal at Midnight
(Student Ghetto, Albuquerque, NM)

Power lines hiss buzz Hendrix
with such a thunderous passion they pull
taut their metal bolts splintering
wood, in hopes they'll crash
kiss waltz the ground beneath them
tempting the rain to ignite

Sometimes the dealers avoid the alleys intentionally
sometimes the buses decide to turn in early taking their work
       home
with them, longing for highway like leaving is muscle memory
morning always bring the reminder that they are chained to the
       city

The garbage man can mimic every lick of a Hendrix cord struck
the garbage man, who is all too aware of the loneliness
all that is forgotten passing through his hands

So we are the ones that are left to rummage through starlight
on another night that's gone dim screaming
that the moon become louder
dreamers searching for salvation in the same places
for something electric and coming up empty

The music caresses every curve of the neighborhood
carries its thickening breath and sings
all of our pain in harmony with the wind purring
against our necks tempting us to ignite

At what point do dreams become bigger
than themselves and instead become the godly
urge of a tired bus hurdling toward destiny?

Where does the music go while the static
fills our ears to busting on the corners of University and Central
Girard and Central
Carlisle and Central
San Mateo and Central
and scatters us murmuring?

You know the rain has never been enough for us
can't you hear it in the writhing of these lines?
the ache in this poem?

Tomorrow the buses will sleep late
the garbage man will remember for the rest of us
and we will remain empty
as ever, scouring those alleys for them dealers
waiting to ignite

Bruce George
I'm in a World

I'm in a world
  of concrete and steel
   of mace and riots
    of endless talk
     of endless plots
      of prison politics
       of taking orders
        of giving orders
         of recycled dreams
          of letters gone unanswered
          of funerals unattended
          of lock-downs
           of beat-downs
           of testosterone
            of claustrophobia
           of anger
            of no love
             of no hope
              of no peace!

I'm in a world

where you look through and not at
where you cry on the inside
where you die on the inside
where you take no prisoners
where you are taken prisoner
where time stands still
where time passes by
where you are forgotten
where you are not forgiven
where you lose your mind
where you lose your soul
yet I'm still a man
yet I'm still human
yet I'm a child of God
yet I'm free!

John Blake
From the Dead, Life.

Black leather jacket, fitted as a title, gray shirt
relaxes on his chest, proud of its wrinkles,
Black Chuck Taylors, leather, tough
as the dried neck of a slave under Georgia sun,
South Carolina humidity, stronger than a Gainesville whip,
taps the rhythm of a march on Birmingham or
calloused feet walking miles during a Selma boycott,

Keb Mo sits in a chair, somewhere in the White House,
film plays witness to hands from Compton as he plays
America The Beautiful on a steel guitar. He smiles, leans
to press his spine against hard wood and resurrects a Jackson
chain gang, and plucks an honest rendition, strings sing tired,
like fingers red from bloodstained thorns and a canvas sack of
         cotton.
Keb, before wearing his suit for the show, blue denim-ed

thump of one leg like the Mississippi rocks against levies,
like Republican fists on podiums, Keb sways his head
and sings Ol' beautiful... his left pinky, adorned in an iron
corset to twang the people's plea, America! America,
and the smile is gone, eyes shut tight as unemployment line
         windows,
foot-tap paced steady with Harriet's walk north, south, north
         again,
guitar coughs memories of mahogany women hanging white
         sheets

cologne-d by smoke.

God shed His grace on thee...
and another skeleton is being found in Haiti,
another house, what's left, bulldozed in the Ninth Ward,

Troy Davis' smile and promise that he's now free,
and my father should have had more opportunity,
and my mother shouldn't have been thrown into
January's Harlem River for loving a Black man,

and Tuskeegee Airmen, and the 54th Regiment of Massachusetts
scream once more before cannons spit on them and the sand
opens to swallow their dreams, a neck snaps beneath magnolias
exploding with Spring how Macy's buys gunpowder
and sprays color across a July 4th sky, and Frederick Douglass
refuses to understand, and Langston's question,
deferred here, before our first Black President and Sojourner-
  dark wife

rock to five-hundred years, Keb's foot taps, once
for every triumph, for every unjust gavel,
for every bone that trapped Nat's sickle,
for each pump behind slave quarters and juke joints,
kilos dropped off in South Central, every shot of heroin
that nodded on Ray's piano and sang through Miles' horn.

From Sea to Shinin' sea…

I weep for a faster tempo.

Dr. Doris Fields

Truth and Reconciliation

to be truthful is to be
free
to become whole is to become
a partner to peace
become   self
love   speak
truth   is to forgive
reconciliation to always go back
honoring
Afrocentric Sankofa

love is deeper than
hate
can exist in the superficiality of being
the periphery   edging out
only

ancient collective African understanding of ancestry
proven via theoretical attachment philosophy
scientific   evidence
that our deepest spiritual being   whole
is love   attachment   via
safety   pin

indeed we are
one
can
survive   with
adoration   care
full   devotional
respect
of self   of one
an   other

holding up
peace
in the face
of conflict   in the practice
truth   a critical necessity
to reconcile the rift
in the valleys of our lives
the crevices of our cultures
the highways of our journeys
in the motor that drives us from here to there
the oil that lubricates the loco motion
in the heart that bleeds
the lips that kiss
the arms that embrace

reconciliation   evolves into
peace   pieces
is the reward for all
lives
in the mending
fissure between
forgiveness and truth

Sonia Sánchez

14 haiku

(for Emmett Louis Till)

1.
Your limbs buried
in northern muscle carry
their own heartbeat

2.
Mississippi . . .
alert with
conjugated pain

3.
young Chicago
stutterer whistling
more than flesh

4.
your pores
wild stars embracing
southern eyes

5.
footprints blooming
in the night remember
your blood

6.
in this southern
classroom summer settles
into winter

7.
i hear your
pulse swallowing
neglected light

8.
your limbs
fly off the ground
little birds . . .

9.
we taste the
blood ritual of
southern hands

10.
blue midnite
breaths sailing on
smiling tongues

11.
say no words
time is collapsing
in the woods

12.
a mother's eyes
remembering a cradle
pray out loud

13.
walking in Mississippi
i hold the stars
between my teeth

14.
your death
a blues, i could not
drink away.

Teresa E. Gallion

Homeless

The evening sits quietly in twilight,
waits for darkness to crush its chest.
You sit at the bus stop
surrounded by wine bottles,

discarded fragments of paper,
a rainbow of trash
waiting for the world to rescue you.
The wind blows trash around feet

barely covered in dirty tennis,
holy like the smallpox.
Inertia still grinding your knees,
you practice your release lines every day,

convinced something will happen.
A stream of light
rips the belly of the street.
Your teeth sparkle in the light.

As your yellow smile grows,
your feet tango in the shadows.
Could that be the reason
you still breathe another day?

E. Ethelbert Miller

Tipping

The tip of my tongue
went looking for you today.

Please Come To My Funeral
I Need To See You

When you left
Wednesday became Tuesday.
I just wanted to start over
(again). Just a conversation
if not forgiveness. Your leaving
is the end of beauty. So much
is broken - even the air is fragile.
Breathing places a knife
near my heart.

Listening   So Close To You

We should never be alone
with just our poems. What is
this caesura   between your
legs? Why does it speak so
loudly   to me?

Jabari Asad

Peter Pan

Walk on clouds and
Break a piece off

Tastes like
Dreams that have yet to be fulfilled

Dance on the still
Surface of a lake
Under the moonlight with
Your shadow
Stretching to the heavens

Teach someone how to fly
It's quite simple

Close your eyes,
stand on your toes,
stretch out your arms,
and exhale

Your breath will carry

Your spirit

To places your body

Could never go

Make peace with your enemies
If you don't have an enemy,

                                        get one

Then make peace with them

It's a magical feeling
To forgive another person
It's even more powerful
When you can forgive yourself

One life to live
so live it well

So well
That when you are reincarnated
You are brought back as a god

Wield perfection
Like it's your own personal katana
Pierce wrong doings
The same way that whispers pierce silence

Commit no acts of violence

Stand on a bridge
Look out over the horizon
Count the water towers
Poking through the treetops

Kick a funky beat box

In honor of the fat boys
If you're too young to remember the fat boys

Then Google that shit!

Recognize the past
Is the easiest way
To move into the future
Try to catch your shadow

A lost boy
Playing in never-never land

Hold on to that innocence
The imagination you used
As a broad sword
To cut down conformity

Be a lost boy forever

Play games, have fun, laugh
Nobody is too cool to laugh

It refills your spirit
Like ambrosia

I will remain a lost boy forever

So if you
Want to join me
Just look towards the second star

                        to the right,

Straight on till morning

Think of a wonderful thought
…and fly

Idris Goodwin

How to say Idris

I always thought it just came out of a book.

My mother still has it
looks home made, the cover
crude and orange

African Names

Inside the book it says something like Idris means ever lasting or
    never to die
Immortal – but I don't think that's right.

My mother Pat, my dad Don, their parents Thelma, James, Ruth
    and also James

Their siblings named Alicia, Ron, Paul, Theresa, Darrin,
    Reginald, Janet, Joyce, Jay, Val, Alvin, James Jr. –– they
    wanted to break the chain

they were afro-wearing 1960's black power children
trying to make a statement through their offspring
wanted us to have names with throat and vowels

In Detroit, they were a minority, our black church asked,

Why you give that boy that African name? that Muslim name?

There are names in the good book — strong Apostle names.

Names in the phone book — strong regular names.

In the suburbs, I was a minority, my white middle American
    school asked,
Is it eye-dris?
IDI-ris?
I'd rice?
Isadore?
Ivan?
Iggy?
Can I just call you I?

Can I call you E?
Can I call you something
other your name?

Age 11, I ask my Mom, can I change my name to something else?
        Tony, Mark, Sean - something else?

Being named Idris in North America will arrest people

You must grow patience.

what an interesting name.
that's so unusual

Sounds Turkish.
Sounds Greek.
Are you Muslim?

Where does it come from?

Age 16 two Arab guys come through my register
get big eyed when they see my name tag.

they're curious
how the name found its way to a Target in suburban Michigan

They're disappointed when I tell them about *African Names*

Age 28 I am in the middle east, where they pronounce it
        beautifully
not all straightened and flattened
E-Dreece

They have given it a joyful bounce.

Idris is a prophet
in the Quran

earlier – Age 20, new to Chicago, broke, cleaning cigarette butts
        out of the restaurant urinal for minimum wage, my boss,
        a giant stereotype with turtle neck, sport coat, big
        glasses, and thick-as-Ditka's-mustache accent – unzips at
        the urinal

(Yep, the one I just cleaned)

He smirks I aint gonna remember that name of yours. How bout
    I just call you Eddie.

And my name became Eddie until his assistant suggested that
    he stop for fear I would claim cultural insensitivity

The gentleman from the UK tells me the Welsh have a myth

There is Morocco's Moulay Idris

The Jazz world's Idris Mohammed

There is the other theater artist Idris Ackamoor

Television's Idris Elba

What does it mean?

Fiery poet – prophetic cashier – confused minority

What does it mean?

confused minority
Black power baby –

It's so exotic
What is it again?

Philosophic cleaner of urinals

I ain't gonna remember that
That's gonna take me a while to learn

old, young, black, white, the spectrum

What does it mean?
How do you say it?

I call myself Idris
like my grandma says it
but who knows if she's saying it right

Suzi Q. Smith

I Do Not Know How to Love You in English

I cannot tell by its rhythm where this heart was born,
it is only music pulsing through palms.
We know this when we hold hands,
let whispers tickle ears
whatever language they assume.

I do not know how to cry in English
     no sé cómo llorar en Español,
tears are born world citizens
they do not need to speak to find each other,
to rush into rivers that cannot be dammed.

I will not ask the wind where it is from.
It would only answer
with its coming and going,
does not recognize these fences or lines,
does not even see them.

I will not ask the Monarchs for a passport,
will not pinch them from the air
and pin them for their passage,
will not shoot them
as they fly away.

I will not shush the roaring seas
beating upon the border from another nation's shore
will not pretend its origin is worth less or more,
we are each of us worth our weight in water
or *en papeles.*

I will not ask each grain of sand
from whence it came,
will not interrogate the sediments
and segregate them by shade,
I will not cast a net around the beaches.

I do not know how to love you in English
  No sé cómo te amo en Español;
only know that all that life begins with love
that cannot be walled or conquered.
I will not ask love where it comes from,

only know that it resides in me,
in the *descansos* dotting the desert.
I do not know what language bullets speak
have only ever heard them whisper past my head
in words I do not wish to remember or repeat,

would rather press palm to palm and whisper poems
"Give us your tired, your poor, your huddled masses
yearning to breathe free . . ."
Would rather smile, warm as stew-filled belly
and break bread.

I will not ask the flames I cook with for identification
when they burn more orange
than red, white, or blue

as I do not know how to eat in English
  No sé cómo comer en Español;

I do not know how to breathe in English
  No sé cómo respirar en Español;

I do not know how to bleed in English
  No sé cómo sangrar en Español;

but I think it is the same
  Creo que es lo mismo

Con mis palabras
y con mi lengua rota
yo trato hablar.

Hakim Bellamy

Cuba, NM

At not a day over 7
Maybe 8
She stood in between the double doors
On display

"Rest stop"
The wrong phrase to use
Cause she was definitely working
The absent smile was proof

Not selling herself
But rather entire generations
Picked, pushed, promised then pulverized
Into precious gems

Worth more when rare
This was her culture
And as she has learned thus far
It is one thing she can sell better than them
The soul she can sell faster than they sold theirs

One thing that they can't take
Only buy

No telling how long she'd been standing there
Before she unreturned my smile
Barely pierced herself,
She hustles ear rings that are not for ceremony
Just tradition

Holds them in arms that say "buy"
But stares at me with eyes that say "go away"
I could tell she'd been standing there

Almost as long as we've been living here
    From the burden of her gait

As she drug herself back to mom's four door office
Cell phone attached to ear
In lieu of product she doesn't sniff
Just like a pimp

On minutes, babygirl
Hasn't worked enough hours to pre-pay yet
But will

And I've seen us sell each other in different forums
Shrink rap ourselves up in marketable art forms
But at least

At at least 7
Maybe 8
Hours on her feet

She put in an honest day's work to sell hers.

Sherod Smallman
360 Degree Hair

"Your hair is so beautiful;
I mean
if my hair could do that I would totally do that"
She meant no harm in this statement
just a curious Caucasian lady admiring something she liked but
        didn't quite understand
And I knew she didn't when she asked "So, how long did it take
        you to grow them"
HHHmmmm good question
Well, let's see
360 years
She looked lost in my answer
What do you mean? Well ….
It took 17 years of looking in the mirror to recognize myself
17 years to love myself
And 21 years to find myself
18 years of hating my skin and 4 years in high school hating
Light skinned Kenny because I wish I could jump into his
16 years of trying brushing my hair into a 360 degree waves and
        good self esteem
16 years to realize that the waves only came crashing on dark
        skin shore
26 years of your hair's so nappy joke
26 years of you're brown skin and handsome too
And 26 years not to give 2 fucks
16 years of putting light skin long hair girls on a trophy shelf
and dark skin girls in the attic
4 years of wearing my Frederick Douglass Fro
to see that dudes were hating cause they don't have the Heart to
        do it.
1 year after I cut my fro
dudes started growing

Side note
I know this is irrelevant
It really is irrelevant
But girls thought it was cute
and braided my fro just for the hell of it
And when I wore my glasses they thought I was so intelligent
I didn't need them then, it just added to the element
which brings me to
11 years being down with natural hair
1 year at an H.B.C.U. to see that being natural doesn't mean
        you're down for shit
5 years of interaction with Afro-centric African Americans
        trying to prove their ethnicity through wrist bangs and
        Malcolm X t-shirts to see that was the extent of their
        revolution
15 years of listening to aunty about good hair
11 years of ignoring her 'cause she's 63 years old from the deep
        south and that's all she knows
24 years to call my hair air condition in summer and a wool cap
        in the winter
24 years of me saying I would never lock my hair
But to answer your question more directly....Miss
It has taken me 6 years to grow branches out of the 360 year old
        tree of my life
360 locked branches that bear the fruit of knowledge that
My students, family, and children will grow from so their roots
        won't start as unhealthy as mines
But enough about me
Nice White lady
How long did it take to grow yours?

Stephen Sargent
Saviors Day

The holy mother gave birth to me
Two continents and a covenant from Bethlehem
7755 miles from Mecca
and an ocean of lifetimes from Jerusalem
I never felt far from God

As I grew older I was taught
about the saviors and prophets
who came to redeem us

I bore witness to a world
crumbling under the weight of inertia
famines
wars
cities falling
and they tell me Christ and Muhammad
ascended to Heaven

There are
14 million practicing Jews
1.5 billion Muslims and
2.1 billion Christians

Approximately 4 billion people in the world waiting for a savior

you can spend your entire life in prayer lines
asking others to read your palms
Only the illiterate cannot read the scripture on their hands
life has taught me the peril of gazing up
while everything around you is avalanching...
all of us are searching
wrap salvation in your own skin

the Dagara of west Africa
Initiate their elders
gift them with ceremonial robes
those most soiled with dirt are viewed as holiest

Live like a dust storm!
God is on the ground,
in the foxholes and trenches,
the alleys,
in the toothless smiles
sleeping in the cardboard condos of your capitals
feed, clothe, build, love, Chrysanthemum

do not shy at the burden of brilliance
some of us have made a science

of self sabotage
it is always easier
to step down
than up

Believing someone else will save you
Is the easy way out

Be yourself
You will not lose your way
you will not drown in it
the diagnose,
the divorce,
the layoffs,
the miscarriage,
the abandonments
you have 4 million pores in your skin
sweat them out

You have 206 bones
a heart
a brain
a spine
you were built for withstanding
You've got 32 teeth minus the breakups and bully's
roll with the punches

write the wrongs from the paragraphs
you have been sentenced to
the lines on your hands
were never meant to remain blank
when you are gone
let them find evidence under your fingernails.
Grind!
do it!
for the lovers and loveless
for the ancestors who wanted to go home
but didn't have the strength
to swim 9 thousand miles

ask her to dance
before the music stops
and her smile fades to disappointment
put the beautiful song on repeat

there is no after-party
we are not auditioning

God is on the ground
with the failures
dirty needles
burning buildings
and malfunctioning rocket-ships

And
they tell me
Christ and Muhammad ascended into heaven
in my book
that makes them more
escape artist
than saviors.
crosses
rosary beads
prayer mats
don't let someone who died 2,000 years ago
come between us.

Muslims pray 5 times a day
Buddhists meditate
Hindus recognize over 330 million manifestations of the divine

Let your sweat outweigh your ceremony
put the beautiful song on repeat
all of us are searching
you will not lose your way

Sonia Sánchez

haiku poem: 1 year after 9/11

Sweet September morning
how did you change skirts so fast?

What is the population of death
at 8:45 on a Tuesday morning?

How does a country become
an orphan to its own blood?

Will these public deaths
result in private bloodletting?

Amongst the Muslim, the Jew, and the Christian
whom does God love more?

How did you disappear, peace, without
my shawl to accompany you?

What cante jondo comes
from a hijacked plane?

Did you hear the galvanized steel
thundering like hunted buffalo?

Glass towers collapsing in prayer
are you a permanent guest of God?

Why do some days wear the
clothing of a beggar?

Where did these pornographic flames
come from, blaspheming sealed births?

Did they search for pieces of life
by fingerprinting the ash?

Death speaking in a loud voice,
are your words only for the deaf?

What is the language for bones
scratching the air?

61

What is the accent of life
when windows reflect only death?

Hey death! You furious frequent flier,
can you hear us tasting this earth?

Did the currents recognize her sound
as she sailed into the clouds?

Does death fly south
at the end of the day?

Did you see the burnt bones
sleepwalking a city?

Is that Moses. Muhammad. Buddha. Jesus.
gathering up the morning dead?

Why did you catch them, death,
holding their wings out to dry?

How did this man become
a free-falling soliloquy?

Why did September come whistling
through the air in a red coat?

How hard must the wind
blow to open our hearts?

How to reconnoiter our lives
away from epileptic dreams?

How to live—How to live
without contraband blood?

Is this only an eastern wind
registering signatures of ash?

Do the stars genuflect
with pity toward everyone?

William Allen, Jr.

Beah Richards—The Beacon of Light, Who Shines So Bright*

Your poignant truths of unblemished words have made
stereotypical lies wish that they had never been heard.

Who are we talking about?
Bee?
No, we ain't talking about "Opie and Aunt Bee."
We're talking about a woman, who brought the *spirit* of
her ancestors from across the sea!

While the world would have preferred for truths of our being to
remain in the twisted and tormented bones on the ocean
floor.

You fought graciously and artistically; and let your words
cascade right up to society's door—not timidly pushing
the door ajar. But you let our ancestral *spirits* move you
on—to act and write of past lives...so near and yet so far.

Mammies, bucks, coons and mulattos are how the cinema and
stage portrayed us to be.
But you would brandish those images, like a woodsman who
cuts down a tree.
Who are you? They would ask!

Beah... Beah Richards!

How we were to be perceived was a correction that was
definitely in order.
You weaved such a sterling life, when you played
in James Baldwin's play, *The Amen Corner.*

You played a mother of understanding. You didn't see your son
  as a sinner;
    when you supported Sidney Poitier—in *Guess Who's*
      Coming to Dinner?

You drove your audiences wild, in your original penetratingly
  profound play—*One Is A Crowd*.

You were tender, touching, sensuously regal, and fashionably
    and politically chic in a role that *you* penned for the
    stage—in your wonderfully earthshaking production of
    A Black Woman Speaks.

You were always a *powerhouse* who projected a character's *true*
    soul.
    Having complexities of layer that you brought to your
      roles.
    Layers of truths that were *seldom*...if ever told.

    And now into infinity... your gifts will forever by our—
    To have and to behold.

You are our Beacon of Light...Who Shines So Bright!

Beah!
Ms. Beah Richards!

-----

* Beah Richards (1920-2000) was an actress on Broadway and
in many films, including "Guess Who's coming to Dinner,"
"Beloved," "Purlie Victorious," "A Raisin in the Sun," "Mahogany,"
"The Miracle Worker," "Drugstore Cowboy," and others. She won
two Emmys and was nominated for a Tony and an Oscar.
The poet wrote, "This poem was written for the late actress
Beah Richards. On April 2, 2000, I received a phone call that

she was ailing badly and I was invited to visit her and say my final goodbyes. Upon my arrival, I was greeted by the noted actress Lisa Gay Hamilton, who was Ms. Richard's caregiver. Ms. Richards sat on her couch, resplendent, radiant, even though she was hooked up to an oxygen tank. I delivered my tribute poem to her in a command performance. I recalled what a trailblazer she had been in the Arts, her many roles, the numerous plays she had performed in, written, taught and directed; a part of her social and Civil Rights activities. I remembered especially her award-winning plays, "One Is A Crowd" and "A Black Woman Speaks," which made our culture richer, and also showed how much more work needs to be done concerning our racial/ cultural/social ills."

assemblage sculpture by William Georgenes

Jane Lipman

Early Morning Magpies,
Evening Deer

This morning's sky—a moth's wing
committing myriad annihilations
of blue.

Spotted towhee, your orange eyes!
the world's secret cause—
but you won't lift them.

To say what one loves, and only that—
as the child who asks, Will the kitty
turn on its motor, please?

My species defies, invites grief.
May we come to compassion, see with eyes
of melting glaciers.

May scholars sawing their ideas
with scrupulosity, obscurity and tang
be smitten by a tree toad chorus.

May the mismatched wife
nursing a cognac
lie down where thyme grows wild.

May self-silenced poets claim
the domain of the fecund
and learn not to forfeit,

even for family
wild plumage or the doe's great eyes.
Give us plum orchard and bean row.

The Muse writes to us in tree bark,
dirt, blushing clouds.
Lightning meanders draw us to their script.

Jane Lipman
Into Your Hands

Into your hands, I deliver this dust, these crumbs,
minty fragrance of crumbled catnip.
Rebuild in humankind
what people have demolished.
Break us like November foliage.

Powdered, be the secret
ingredient spread imperceptible
over and into everything.
Cast off your veils as the corn does.
In this emptiness, what is your
Viking name? Be Word,
symbol of a world.

Be tracks that disappear in the wind.
Circle inside the spiral.
Be still at the heart
of the story that's spinning.
Live vertically.

Jane Lipman

What the White Swan Said

In the glory
of its gliding
a white swan crosses
the night lake—

sails resplendent
into the middle
of our kiss.

Suddenly I find myself
in the center of a gaze.
I am a fulcrum, she says
an occasion for rejoicing.

Yes! my heart cries—
I didn't know swans swim at night.

I don't just love light, she replies.
I can see the color, blind,
that swallows all other color.

And I can smell grief.

You have a hole in your heart,
truthfully, several.
I've come to heal one….

The niece who longed to be your daughter,
who loved horses, and ice cream
and a clay squirrel—

your beloved girl—
after two marriages and two children
breast cancer stalked her…

and you walked
with her towards death…
at whose deathbed you stayed
breathing with her

counting the seconds
      as they increased
      between breaths
      comforting her through pain
      on the in-breath
      guiding to choose the clear light
      on the out-breath

the one whose burial
you long to redo.

Right there and then
under the gaze of the swan
I release Lisa, my very dear,
from ten years
inside that opulent
coffin, its lining
of pleated pink satin,
cold steel handles—

I stroke and loosen
the matronly hairdo
concocted
by make-up artists of the dead—
free her hair
and her beauty—

lay her out in blossoms and starlight
in soft grass by the lake.
Ask her, Should the swan be willing,

would you like her to sail you
to the next world?

The white swan queries,
How do you know
the dead aren't happy?

How do you know I'm not
the daughter of your heart—
interrupting your
kiss
to have your attention
once more?

Kyle Laws
Port-au-Prince to Montrouis
June 2010

Rows of men, some one-handed,
        offer to carry bags
to a Toyota Landcruiser

Every inch of open land
        outside airport
covered with tents, mostly blue

"1,500,000 homeless,"
        says Roger Jean-Charles,
"300,000 in Gonaives"

Smell of charcoal is Haiti I know
        and behind block walls
laced in garbage, more tents

We follow weighed-down *tap-tap**
        Jan in front seat with Max
me in back with Marckenson

Cloud-striped sun sets
        on wooden frames draped
in white canvas, blue nylon

Sunday play at soccer field entrance
        reminds of Japanese
internment camp outside Granada

Metal Quonset huts gone
        junipers growing up
through slab foundations

Beginning of smell of sea
        as we head to Montrouis
banana truck picking up passengers

Denuded slopes of chalk
        roll into green hills
then a cool breeze

New pastel housing deeper in tones
        than mausoleums
overturned in cemetery

Azul, deep rose and gold
        of plaster walls
that I wanted to save on Grand

As section of adobe wall
        open for inspection
in Palace of Governors in Santa Fe

Fields of banana trees
        not here 2 years ago
or scent of fish in fire smoke

---

tap-tap=Haitian public buses

Kyle Laws
Saint-Marc to Gonaives
Monday 7 A.M. June 2010

Stop-lighted intersection
motorbikes, bicycles, wheelbarrows
uniformed children on way to school
Toyota follows *tap-tap* burning oil
corn on cab for market
swerving for dead cow in road

Goats sun on pale turquoise
& pink mausoleums
flooded cinderblock foundations
stagnant sheen of grey-blue

Beginning of rice country
lunch tied in tree
heads bandana-ed pink & orange
hoes and backs to irrigated field

Helmeted soldiers in white U.N. truck
white cormorants in dried paddy
beaks down
bony burros
crypts with crosses
broken bottles cemented atop walls
teeth loosening drive
jaw aches
going to pave all the way to Gonaives

Jack Hirschman
The Boozhoo* Arcane

For Aja Couchois Duncan

1.

A leather window in Oraibi
flapping in the plateau winds:
poor, poor, poorest of the poor.

These bones of corn scattered
which the snout of a mutt
rummages through

and the bedrock face of this old
anasazi woman grand canyons
deep with echoes.

They came down from the hills
of San Francisco and moved
among the caves along the Beach.

Their skin painted a red tobacco
color, with feathers and foxtails
and arrowheads adorning.

The Kachinas kept multiplying
around them, the sun turned into
a drum pounding out thunder.

Rain weeping out loud, adobe
hanging like tiers of tears
iwah yagagah wiya annikyaati

Hio hio hiovi: Morning dove cry.
Mimi paguwixi: You fish vagina.
Mimi umiwanti: You sibling of

invisibles. *Mimi paga arayumengki:*
You kicker against the riverbank
because the purple water of the

rainbow has turned muddy, because
the moon has died. Rise up Rise up,
Spirit Mountain: *kitikiyikwitikiy Aagah.*

Rise up Rise up: *Kitikiiyikwitikiy*
Morning star: *Tasiantipu utsivi.*
Now you hear me simply. What's

a revolution without the spirit of a
people? Between any two
instances a light subsists. What's its

name? Who's its transmitter? Why
when it's so simple do we have to
make like we don't hear it simply?

I am Momo, the Bee Kachina.
I go from ear to ear, putting
honey of the people everywhere.

O forget about whether your
initials stand up. In eternity
they're drunken. Yipahoo!

In eternity, people are flying
around inside birds
and the rivers have wings.

2.

The night fire warm in the stillness
with only the muffled crackling
of the flames...What is to write?

A journey without years and all the
thrums of music come to this.
Joy in what there is of breath and

flame and ink-like streaks of its being
set upon paper. I learned tonight at
winter solstice The Dipper, The Twins

and as far as Shakbazian—all of them
could be light as cottonwood roots you
in the mind of my hand----no effigy

but the myriad play of the spirit dance.
    wa   hi   hi   hi   hi
    wa   hi   hi   hi

75

Brave warriors, where have you gone?
ho   kwi   ho   ho
ho   kwi   ho   ho

And so they sang in Minnesota when
John Kakagreesick died at 124
and Ted Mahto could write of how it is

not knowing who one is or if one is
when usurocracy has made a Thunderbird
or a Pinto with more power than a horse.

Woodlands, where the *oshki anishanaabe*
strung their shells by the river-rapids
among loon and bear and beaver:

May whoever sings after the mystery of
Ojiibikan carry the tones
Wa hi hi hi/ ho kwi ho ho

We are not a tape deck of cards.
At *Nahgahnub,* the feather's end,
the feather regenerates.

I am Little Cough. I am sienna. I am
snowflake on the skin of the evening.
I am inside the belly kiva.

I am already and not yet. I am that small
like a thunderbird design on a fingernail.
I am living *kopavi,* the soft spot, the open

door inside the middle of your forehead,
sitting on the floor looking up the ladder
at the hole in the sky.

3.

kaaaaaaa   shtammmmm   iiiiiiinnnnn ya
kaaaaaaa   shtammmmm   iiiiiiinnnnn ya
xikxikxika xikxikxika   xikooxikoo yo

Descends the Wet Tobacco Kachina, tears
of all the tribes upon him, head half-sun
half-moon, red twins for eyes, blue arms

outstretched, fingers painted maize and green,
a smile upon his face made of two runaway
mustangs kissing the horizon.

I grow up to greet him: *Boozhoo!* I grow a
womb like a drum. I make the world in
the sand around him. Feathers grow from

his thumbs. I feel the end of the blood and
the beginning of good rain when I near the
deep nightshade, an aroma of a hundred trees.

And he takes off his skin and covers us both
with it like the wet blanket of my fears like
the wet blanket of our years, saying:

When it is dried we'll smoke it and name it
Where We Came Together. So sound
the split-stick clacker, the *mawuwi* like a

jew's harp, the six-holed *ya'lu* fluted, and
the whistles made of swan-bone—-who
had no war dance in their ceremony.

Can you touch, can you tickle each other?
cykycyky   cykycyky   cykycyky
like the bristling of a meadowlark through

the blue dusk of the branches, this pure ridge
of many strains, *copastram* and *zengo*, svastikas
whirling counter-clockwise to the spiral Christ

in the heart of the Davidian star. Can you put
nations together from the fragments of dispersion
and exploitation? Know that before even Oraibi

Amerinds dreamed these many wanderers from
big city or metropolis, crack minds that wanted
to wear the silken snake of the Yuba, build

as though a hunk of wood were a speaking tree,
speak hip argot, hoot coyote and even redneck
at the mouth's corner, only to be

dug into the plot, to a plot of soil, weaving each
other's visits, spinning the clay of the whirling sun
and talking to the animals made of stars at night

scattered these many nations held in the derringer-
shaped counties of the red palm's reflection.
How many reincarnations ago? How many

hummingbirds forming a feather of smoke from the
pipe of that river-mouth? Ohlone here oh alone
along the extant streets in the soft arrow of memory.

Who says 1935 was the last of the you? Look at how
lazy I am when work is done, how I love to look
at the different birds, or play my flute or look up

words that the trees list leaf by leaf, like a loafy poet
with nothing but nature on his mind. It can take me
ten San Francisco eons to lift my hand and wipe the

sunlight out of my eyes, that deep sienna red-purplish
and liquid amber glow which Whiteman Sanfrancisco
knows for 10 minutes but which Ohlone, because

we invented it, breathes all night long without needing
a picture of, or taking an elevator to, it, which is the
etheric aura of *Awwir* and *Tawa,* the founders of light.

Boozhoo is an Ojibwe word meaning *Greetings!*

Janet Eigner
Assisted to Italy Two

Mother's left the building again to search
for her husband, a year ago passed on,
says, "Do you know where Len's gone?"

"Our charter...we can't
guard her safely on this side,"
worries the director,
"Call in our movers."

We creep along the palm-shaded sidewalk
the pristine lawns, behind the scrawny,
muscled couple toting
the plaid sofa-bed, her queen mattress
sturdy chair with arms to push herself upright
cherry china cabinet to hold the proud evidence
they'd shed the immigrants' threadbare cloth:
Lalique crystal sculpture, a sixty year collection:
sister takes the small dove.
I warm the smaller owl in my palm

across the parking lot that divides each
past day lived in her vivid suite,
front door open to clan and friends,

to the stuccoed,
sprightly-muraled building,
discreet lock on the fire door
behind the front desk and another
barring the clinic's medicine pantry.

The residents, sorted
by their stage of decline
live in pods: Tuscany, Stratford,
names that might nudge their lives' past –
Windsor, Bellagio, Loire –
regions that might root and comfort the aging

children
that their own world's not yet shuttered.

The elevator hums us
to Italy Two, her one bright room.
She still knows us, her heart-aching children, says,
"this room is fine for you two,
but time for me to go back home."

She's just halfway to
her next destination.

Debbi Brody
Ode to Chile

The world, upside down,
clouds wear crinoline rivulets
on the bottom, flat on top.

Yesterday two Red Fox
today, four Andean Condors.

Life begins in calcium carbonate,
God lives in photosynthesis.

There are still one or two *Anorak**
words with us, *paine** means blue.

A "Hello Kitty" sticker on the bronze
rib cage at the unknown Indian's tomb.

If O'Keeffe had lived in Patagonia
the *cerros** and *Guanaco** skulls
would have revolutionized Chilean art.

Cross *El Estrecho de Magallanes,**
*Tierra del Fuego** on the right,
the world's southern most city on the left.

69,000 *pinguino** couples nest
with their 69,000 fledglings.

First sizable anti-Pinochet protest, a walk
from Neruda's burnt house to his grave.

*Memento Vivere**
live for today
and remember to live.

Anorak=a term for indigenous Patagonians; *cerros*=hills; *paine*="Blue", in
the *Anorak* language, their only surviving word; this area has Chile's
Torres del Paine National Park, with its alpine scenery; *El Estrecho de
Magallanes*=The Straits of Magellan; *pinguino*=penguin; *Memento Vivere*
is Latin, on a plaque at Neruda's northern home; *Tierra del Fuego*=large
island at the tip of South America, divided between Chile and Argen-
tina, with the world's southern-most city, Ushuaia (which is Argentine).

The Choreography of 13 Tangos and 300 Stanzas

by Gary L. Brower

Álvaro Cardona-Hine writes poetry and prose, creates beautiful paintings, composes music, is politically to the Left, and likes to smoke a good cigar. He and his wife Barbara, who also creates beautiful paintings, have studied Zen Buddhism together for many years. In fact, Álvaro is a *sensei*, a lay teacher. They have lived for decades now in the little village of Truchas, on the high road from Santa Fe to Taos, and have a gallery and studio there. The fact is that Álvaro (born 1926 in Costa Rica) is some sort of "Renaissance Man," with multiple talents as a writer, a visual artist and a composer.

In his award-nominated book which chronicles his adolescent years in Los Angeles, **Thirteen Tangos for Stravinsky** (Santa Fe, Sherman Asher, 1999), Cardona-Hine presents the reader with a personal history: his family had come to the U.S., his father named Consul for Costa Rica in Los Angeles, and they stayed. He remembers an idyllic early childhood in Central America, then moving to southern California.

Álvaro grew into a man and an artist in Los Angeles, and while there, he met Gene Frumkin. They remained friends for more than 50 years (until the death of the latter). As poet V. B. Price says in his foreword to **The Curvature of the Earth** (UNM Press, 2007), in which Álvaro and Gene published their poetry after a joint trip to Spain, "They met in Los Angeles during the McCarthy Era where they were part of the Los Angeles poetry world with the likes of Tom McGrath, Bert Meyers, Charles Bukowski, Mel Weisburd, and many others. . . . Both men were central to a long neglected poetic movement of social awareness and humane conscience originating in Los Angeles in the 1950s and 1960s during and after the House Un-American Activities Committee purged Southern California schools and the motion picture industry of socially concerned writers, actors and teachers." (p.xi).

This was an era that now has unfortunately been forgotten (or repressed), a period of Right-Wing attacks on the political Left, and Progressive causes, as well as on the American political system itself. It was led by Republican U.S. Senator Joe McCarthy of Wisconsin, abetted by FBI Director J. Edgar Hoover, and some conservative Democratic Senators. During the McCarthyite era in the late 1940s and 1950s, attacks were made against Jews, gays, liberals, intellectuals, professors, universities, artists, leftists. Anti-intellectualism, homophobia and anti-Semitism were important factors in motivating the Right Wing, in addition to a "Power Grab". They were only defeated when they overplayed their hand and the public turned against them, as did moderate members of their own party, when they attacked Republican President Eisenhower as a traitor and the U.S. Army as infiltrated by gays and leftists. Many of the congressional hearings were broadcast nationally on television like "Show Trials" in dictatorial societies. McCarthy held up false lists of supposed leftists and gays who he claimed were everywhere, undermining American democracy. The main tactic was to exercise control through fear and when that didn't work, to persecute and prosecute those who wouldn't be cowed, in what came to be called the "Red Scare."

Many famous writers, actors, film directors, and others were blacklisted, hundreds were jailed, and an estimated 10,000-12,000 lost their jobs as a result of his "witch hunts." A few of those attacked during this period include: writers Langston Hughes, Nelson Algren, Berthold Brecht, Dashiell Hammitt, Arthur Miller, Dalton Trumbo, Lillian Hellman, Dorothy Parker, Howard Fast, William L. Shirer, Arthur Laurents; screenwriters including the "Hollywood Ten" who refused to testify and were convicted of "contempt of Congress"; actors & directors Charlie Chaplin, Lena Horne, Gypsy Rose Lee, Zero Mostel, Paul Robeson, Edward G. Robinson, Martin Ritt, Burgess Meredith, Jules Dassin, Joseph Losey, Ruth Gordon, Delores del Rio, Lauren Bacall, Humphrey Bogart, Danny Kaye; composers Aaron Copeland and Ira Gershwin; musician Artie Shaw; atomic physicist J. Robert

Oppenheimer; Nobel laureate Linus Pauling; the elderly W.E.B. DuBois; and so many more.

Among the many artists who were called to "testify" before the House Un-American Activities Committee (HUAC) or its Senate counterpart was poet and WWII veteran Tom McGrath (1916-1990). He was at the center of the poetry group which included Gene Frumkin and Álvaro Cardona-Hine. McGrath quite rightly refused to cooperate with the Committee and was fired from his teaching job at Los Angeles State College. (This resulted in protests by hundreds of students and supporters.) Group member Don Gordon, who wrote for the movie studios, was fired and blacklisted. Edwin Rolfe, another of this group, had fought against Franco and his fascist allies in the Spanish Civil War (1936-39) which presaged WWII. (Numerous American volunteer veterans from the anti-Fascist side in that conflict were later persecuted by McCarthy, the FBI, and "conservatives" who often had been supporters and sympathizers of Hitler and Mussolini before WWII.)

In her book **Poets of the Non-Existent City**, subtitled "Los Angeles in the McCarthy Era" (UNM Press, 2002), Estelle Gershgoren Novak notes that "Poetry and politics were closely entwined for the poets who had been affected by the Depression and World War II." Both Cardona-Hine and Frumkin were a part of this poetry scene, which was growing in Los Angeles in tandem with the better-known one in San Francisco. Tom McGrath was the Wizard of this Oz. As Gershgoren explains, however, it wasn't only McGrath's classes, it was his charisma and other attributes that allowed him to create a community of poets, a critique group that became much more than its origins. The two best literary journals of the time were *California Quarterly* and *Coastlines*. Gene Frumkin became editor of the latter. Álvaro was published in both. Of course they printed work of the entire group, including a portion of McGrath's most famous poem "Letter to an Imaginary Friend" (a book-length work of around 100 pages, see the Copper Canyon edition, 1990).

Why is Tom McGrath not better known in American poetry circles? As is the case with many, if not most, American poets of the Left, McGrath's work has largely been ignored by the "literary establishment" because it is controversial. Regarding McGrath's work, poets Kenneth Rexroth and Diane Wakoski have written about this intentional ignorance of his work (See the Poetry Foundation online essay on McGrath). Terence Des Pres, in *Triquarterly*, said, "In American poetry he is as close to Whitman as anyone since Whitman himself..." (Idem.).

McGrath came from a family of North Dakota farmers who suffered like many others during the Depression, spending a portion of his youth riding the rails illegally and hitchhiking around the country to find work. After WWII, where he served in the Aleutian Islands, he won a Rhodes Scholarship to Oxford University, returning to the U.S. in the late 1940s. Poet Sam Hamill has referred to McGrath as "...a Rhodes Scholar who was also a road scholar." Álvaro Cardona-Hine wrote of McGrath's work in the **North Dakota Quarterly** (where McGrath himself had published many works): "What is obvious to the careful reader is that *nothing is missing* from the man's range. It is sage and innocent, canny, detailed and in flight, sensual, fulminating, apparent, immanent, sacred... a true poet, not a propagandist and his work will live because it resonates with a thousand surprising innuendoes of an inner life beyond politics, beyond experience itself." (Ibid.). Not all of McGrath's poetry was political of course. But there are political poems, such as "A warrant for Neruda" or "Against the False Magicians" in which he speaks of the political poem: "It is the poem provides the proper charm,/..../to bring to dance a stony field of fact/and set against terror exile or despair/the rituals of our humanity." (**New & Selected Poems,** Alan Swallow, 1964, p. 94).

McGrath wasn't happy in Los Angeles after he was attacked by HUAC and lost his teaching position, and finally moved back to his home state. He taught at North Dakota State University, then returned to his alma mater, Moorhead State University in Minnesota, where he stayed until retirement in 1983.

Álvaro Cardona-Hine also moved to Minnesota for a while (in the Minneapolis area). In his poem, "Farewell to *Nuestra Señora de Los Angeles,*" he says, "I am abandoning you Los Angeles/.../I am pulling up roots/.../you nearly killed me/made me nine years ballast/in the hold of an insurance company/two years a salesman in the streets/seven at the trough of pornography/ the only free time were those five days/in jail for speeding/Los Angeles/you looked the other way while I/scribbled haiku on the thin edge/of a dime." He travels eastward through Arizona, then New Mexico, where he stopped to see Frumkin on his way north: "Los Angeles you abandoned me through my pores/now the road/like a snake/has bitten my blood." When Álvaro finally got close to his destination, he said, "an hour before Minneapolis/two pheasants cross the road/.../a birthday gift to me at forty nine/seven cycles of seven implicating/a centricity/a tender/complex case." Frumkin (who had been making a living editing a trade paper in LA) accepted a poetry position at the University of New Mexico where he replaced Robert Creeley (who left for SUNY Buffalo). And finally, Álvaro also moved to New Mexico, to the ancient village Truchas.

In the 1960s, Cardona-Hine began to study Zen Buddhism, and it eventually had an effect on his art, in his paintings, and in his writing. **The Gathering Wave (**1961) became very famous in the specialized field of Japanese haiku. This was shortly after the popular paperback by Harold G. Henderson, **An Introduction to Haiku** (Doubleday, 1958), which for many Americans was the origin of their knowledge of the short verse form. Henderson's book, R.H. Blyth's many volumes, and Cardona-Hine's tome established haiku in American poetry as a familiar form. Today, the haiku is well known among American poets, even while the authentic form is frequently misunderstood.

Widespread in the American culture is the idea that anything small or short has lesser importance. Perhaps because we are a large nation, we have an attitude that larger entities, of any type,

86

are more appropriate to the US. The values of quantity and quality are confused: "Bigger is better."

Likewise, lack of knowledge of foreign literature is the norm. Many American poets regard haiku as lacking importance; it is seen as "cute" and a "joke." Nothing so small could have significant meaning. The form involves much more than most people suspect. The haiku is actually very difficult to create and, with its clear poetic surface, depends partly on the ripples of meaning that move outward from the central image into the poem's psychic structure. Dismissal of the form because of brevity is based on ignorance. Unfortunately, this is often also true of acceptance of the form, at least in some Western literary circles. See the first chapter of my **Japanese Haiku in Spanish-American Poetry**, (1966) for a discussion of haiku aesthetics and poetic devices.

In Japanese culture, everything is on a different scale: every Japanese garden is seen not only for what it shows above ground, but for the garden's creator, what he placed below ground. The scale of everything is important because this is a society that lives on a series of islands that limit not only the landmass available but the psychological terrain of an entire culture. Haiku is not a *bonsai* form of poetry. But *bonsai* can be an example of how less can be more, or how the microcosm can imply the macrocosm. Japan also has a different set of aesthetic categories, at least traditionally. Before the arrival of the Europeans, the classical Japanese haiku was developed out of the longer Tanka form and unrelated to the Western Rationalist tradition (which we inherited from ancient Greeks). Rather, the haiku expressed Zen's focus on the paramount value of instantaneous perception based on intuition, a synthesis, as opposed to a lengthy rationalist analysis which takes segments apart to understand the whole. It has been said that the reason for the limit of 17 syllables is that, although it may be an arbitrary number, it is an imagined limit of the human brain before the rational side takes over. Haiku is especially focused on Nature, or humans as an integral part of, and existing on the same level as, all living things. In Rationalist thought we are separated from Nature, in a subjective-objective dichotomy, which gives us the Western tendency of trying to dominate Nature. In classical Japanese haiku, Culture and Nature are brought together at a nexus of the poet's perception, with the emphasis on the Natural. As Basho once said: "When we observe calmly, we realize that every object in nature has its fulfillment."

The question is, how do you transfer a poetic form from one culture to another without destroying it, yet make it understandable to those who learn of it from a different perspective? If you discard all Japanese aspects of the form, you have something that is not related to haiku. This is what many, if not most, "Western" poets have done, which is why the only thing they understand is the traditional haiku length. However, the form limits are simply the "outside husk" of the poem, a part, but not all. What is needed is to keep what *can* be kept from the classical Japanese haiku and joining it to "Western" poetic devices that will work naturally with the two literary traditions, creating a hybrid of sorts, of the best of both worlds. (This means no abstractions, no intense personal emotions, and the experience in the haiku should be identical with that of the poet, no invented situations, for example). What Álvaro did in his book of haiku, **The Gathering Wave**, is to find precisely that balance of the haiku form as a valid poetic structure between both cultures. For example:

Looking at the moon The gathering wave
suddenly remembering sandpipers venturing in
to look at the moon among the children

It is obvious that the poet's study of Zen Buddhism brought him to the poetic place where he could write these haiku in a hybrid form that has the afore-mentioned balance. The second haiku gives the reader an image that is the "humans as a part of nature" focus, and the first is clever in that it refers to what happens in the poet's mind as he looks at the moon, which makes his mind wander, then comes back to his original focus.

Álvaro Cardona-Hine is still painting, composing music, and writing as well as smoking an occasional cigar. And he has some poems about certain artworks he especially appreciates.

In his 2006 Spanish-language volume of poetry *Sucursal de estrella* **(Star Subsidiary),** for example, he has dedicated a poem to Picasso's etching titled "Minotauromaquia" (1935) which shows Europa, the mythological bull. The picture tells a story in a one-frame etching, a somewhat traditional but mythic story. A recent series of paintings uses Egyptian deities such as Isis and Osiris, and another series uses scenes of Buddhist teachers; the viewer sees mythic figures that seem both ancient and modern at the same time. They incarnate the value of tradition in balance with the renewal of the contemporary. Just like the old village of Truchas where Álvaro and Barbara live, with their beautiful contemporary gallery. Just like their art, in all its forms. Just like the haiku of their life, remembering the moon.

The Curvature of Consciousness:
An Interview with Álvaro Cardona-Hine

by George Kalamaras

Álvaro Cardona-Hine, left, with George Kalamaras

I first met Álvaro Cardona-Hine several years ago, and we have kept company with one another since. Our relationship from the beginning has been inextricably intertwined with our mutual friend, poet Gene Frumkin. For years, Gene had told me about Álvaro, from when they first met in Los Angeles in 1957. Gene's Albuquerque home on Mesa Verde NE even housed some of Álvaro's remarkable paintings. Who was this mysterious man—I had often wondered on my pilgrimages to see Gene—who was not only a master poet but painter? It was indeed on one of our visits to see Gene that my wife, Mary Ann, and I first met Álvaro, though oddly enough not at Gene's. As we were leaving the area, another friend, Arthur Sze, suggested over breakfast, quite by chance, that we visit Álvaro in the small mountain village of

Truchas, through which we would be passing on our return to Colorado. Here, Álvaro and his wife Barbara own and operate the Cardona-Hine Gallery, as they have for nearly twenty-five years. Both are painters and poets. Álvaro is also a composer and Zen priest. At 85, perhaps not unlike the Chinese poets of antiquity, he has chosen the solitude of his mountain over the busyness of the world (as the T'ang Dynasty poet Wang Wei describes, "In late years, I love only the stillness").

This constellation of circumstances brought Mary Ann and me (and our then-constant companion, our beagle, Barney) to Álvaro's and Barbara's door. When I mentioned Gene upon our arrival, we were welcomed—quite literally—with open arms (they even welcomed Barney, although their former bulldog, Pushkin, was less than enthusiastic to have our little hound on his turf!). Knowing Álvaro and Barbara now as I do, I suspect we would have been greeted just as warmly without the password "Gene." Still, Gene provided a point of mutual connection, though we soon found that our practice of poetry and interest in the Eastern Wisdom traditions (Álvaro's and Barbara's in Zen, and Mary Ann's and mine in Hindu-yogic meditation) gave us equally rich points of convergence.

What I found in Álvaro was a man of profound generosity who heartily welcomed us and who shared similar poetic influences as I, such as César Vallejo, Miguel Hernández, and the Chinese poets of antiquity.

What I found was a man of humility (so much so that I am careful, now, to temper my praise).

What Mary Ann and I found in Álvaro and Barbara was the kind of friendship for which one can only hope with those rare few among the many one chances to meet.

Before long, Álvaro and I collaborated on two books, a co-authored volume of poetry, **The Recumbent Galaxy** (2010), winner of the C & R Press Open Competition, which also included several reproductions of his paintings, as well as a small collection of my poems, **Something Beautiful Is Always Wearing the**

Trees (Stockport Flats, 2009), made all the more beautiful by a series of paintings Álvaro produced to accompany the verse.

It was several years after that first meeting, during a trip to read with Álvaro from **The Recumbent Galaxy** at Gary Wilkie's and Marilyn Stablein's Acequia Booksellers in Albuquerque in July 2010, that this interview took place. Mary Ann, our young, rambunctious beagle, Bootsie, and I spent the day before the reading (which happened to be Bootsie's birthday) hanging out in Truchas with Álvaro, Barbara, their two young bulldogs, Chocho and Tula, and their cat, Gaia. It was one of those magical days in which one feels the commingling of one's animal, human, and eternal selves, a convergence in which friends catch up on the spoken and unspoken intermingling of their lives. After an invigorating afternoon and a sumptuous supper that Barbara had prepared and left simmering on the stove for us as she headed off to a Zen intensive, we retired to the living room of their adobe home and turned on the tape recorder, letting things unfold from there.*

I am grateful to Álvaro for his patience with my many questions, allowing our conversation to unwind naturally into the organic shape of good talk and the connection of common words and love.

---

* Grateful acknowledgment to Joyce Jenkins for her long hours of work in transcribing the interview.

George Kalamaras: *Thanks for doing this interview, Álvaro. One of the things that I'm interested in is that you're in a unique position as a bilingual speaker and poet. I was wondering if you could talk a bit about the impact of coming to the United States as an immigrant and how that has played out, not only to your sense of being a poet, but moving back and forth between languages as a poet, since you write in both.*

Álvaro Cardona-Hine: Okay, I'll probably ramble a little bit, but let me say to begin with that I was twelve or thirteen when my parents decided to come to this country. My father was appointed consul in California. And my grandmother who lived and was raised in a private college in San Francisco began to teach me a little English—me and my sister—just enough to say "hello" or, you know, a few words. By the time we came I had to face the fact that I had to learn a new language. It took me roughly five years 'til I was eighteen to really master English enough to begin to write poetry. The reason I began to write poetry was because the five years had been a little bit difficult for me. I became very lonely; I didn't have friends because I didn't have the language, but I come from a literary family. My grandfather, my uncle, my father himself, an older brother who's ten years older—a half-brother, Alfredo Cardona-Peña—were poets. So it became logical for me to take my loneliness and put it into literature, into words, into poetry. But it was a struggle at first to know who I was in a different milieu, in a different environment, and the poetry that I began to write for the first five or ten years was a little exaggerated, a little bit unmanageable, and it took the friendship of Gene Frumkin, Mel Weisburd, Stanley Kiesel, Bert Meyers—a few other poets like that—where we shared poetry and were critical of each other to learn how to really avoid the typical beginner's mistakes. So, it took me, probably, until the age of twenty-seven or thirty to really begin to have my own voice.

GK: *And those early poems were in English or in Spanish?*

ACH: They were in English. My Spanish poetry came later when I realized that I had that tradition to follow also, and I was of course in love with the poetry of the generation of the beginning of the twentieth century in Spain: [Miguel de] Unamuno,

93

[Federico] García Lorca, and [Antonio] Machado, and all those poets.

GK: *Well, you mentioned Gene Frumkin and Mel Weisburd, and actually, that was the next question I wanted to ask. You were good friends with the late, great, Thomas McGrath, and you were also a part of this group of poets—Gene among them, Mel, Bert Meyers. Can you say a little about how you met those poets and how you met Thomas McGrath? I'm curious what was the impact of Tom McGrath on you as a poet—I mean not only his poetry but his presence?*

ACH: Yes. To begin with, I have to retract a little bit. At the age of eighteen I also went to college, where I met my first wife, but I also met a fellow named Stanley Kurnik. Actually, I knew him from high school, and we both began to study music together. Stanley was very instrumental in my life, a very powerful influence. A very intelligent boy. He's dead now. He died in a car accident. He wrote poetry in a very traditional style, which eventually led to our disagreement over poetry and the end of our friendship. The friendship was very vital in the early years, and, in fact, up to the middle of my life. He introduced me to McGrath when I came back from Washington State where I was living with my wife and the first two children that I had.

GK: *This would have been 1957, maybe?*

ACH: About 1957, exactly. You're right. So, I came to L.A. and joined Stanley Kurnik's poetry workshop at the First Unitarian Church, which was a very left-wing outfit.

GK: *He was teaching the workshop?*

ACH: He was teaching the workshop, and I joined it just to read my poetry and share ideas and so forth. Very soon after that, he introduced me to Tom McGrath, because Tom McGrath had expressed interest in my work from a little booklet that Stanley had published. He had liked my work, so Stanley felt that he could introduce me to Tom. Well, right away, Tom and I became very, very good friends. He was instrumental in getting me published—in publishing my first book of poetry—which was a book of haiku called **The Gathering Wave.** He asked Alan Swallow, who was his publisher, to publish me, and he published it. Then he [Swallow] subsequently published another book, **The Flesh of Utopia.** So, McGrath was instrumental in helping me shape up as a serious poet—as a poet like he was a poet. Before that, when you're a boy, when you're a teenager, you're writing poetry because you're in love, or you're writing poetry because that's a thing to do chemically, but you're not a poet yet, you know? Unless you're a guy like that Frenchman. What was his name? The young man.

GK: *Oh, not Rimbaud, but…*

ACH: Rimbaud! Yeah, I'm thinking of Rimbaud. My god, what a miracle.

GK: *Right, fifteen. So, if I might interrupt for a second, I'd like to ask about that. My understanding has always been that it was the economy and brevity of your verse that McGrath was initially drawn to. Was it, or what quality do you think it was?*

ACH: No, the little book that Stanley Kurnik published did not have any haiku because I hadn't written haiku yet, but had very vivid imagery, and McGrath liked it. I can show you the book if I can find it, but that's up to you. So, it was a vividness, a freshness, in my attempt to write poetry that he liked right away. And, as a matter of fact, when we met, I told him that I was beginning to write some ideas and calling them "open songs," and he said, "Oh, god, that's a great title! I'd love to use that," and I said, "You can have it!" Subsequently, he wrote a lot of little poems, and I went in the direction of the real haiku, which is five-seven-five syllables, because I felt anything else is telegraphic, and for me, it doesn't work. If you're going to write succinctly you'd better have a form that can back you up. So, my first book was haiku in the traditional Japanese style of five-seven-five syllables, whereas Tom McGrath never went for that and wrote a number of wonderful little poems in a free style.

GK: *Whenever I talk to people who know your work, they tend to know that book, that first Alan Swallow book,* **The Gathering Wave,** *and they say, "Álvaro was really instrumental to me forty years ago. I was*

*reading his haiku, I was reading his short poems." How did you first
come to that form? It doesn't sound like you came to it through McGrath.*

ACH: Not through McGrath, no. It was in Ellensburg, where I
was living, because that's where my first wife lived, and we had
been in Mexico escaping the McCarthy era, and then her mother
got ill, so she came back to the States and got a job, but then we
found out she was pregnant, so I had to leave Mexico and come
back. I got a job at a college there, and not teaching, but working
in the maintenance department. And there I met some students
who showed me a book of haiku by [R.H.] Blyth—the transla-
tions by Blyth. I just couldn't believe the beauty of the work. So it
sunk into me. Something trickled in that affected my aesthetics,
and from then on I began to study Zen, as a matter of fact.

GK: *You had not studied Zen prior to coming into contact with haiku?*

ACH: No, and not with Tom.

GK: *So, haiku, Tom McGrath, and then Zen.*

ACH: Right. And McGrath, when we talked about Zen subse-
quently, he told me a nice anecdote about himself. He said that
one day he was sitting with a Zen master in Little Tokyo, and the
Zen Master said you don't need to study Zen; you have it, any-
body has it, there's no need to study it. This is from a Master.
It freed McGrath from the necessity of pursuing it even more
traditionally or more fully. I, instead, when I met Gisele Cheney,
left my family, lived with her for a couple of years, and went
into Zen with her. By then I was very serious about it, and I had
influenced her into the idea of going into Zen. She was search-
ing for something. She became, subsequently, a great Master:
Prabhasa Dharma Roshi. Let's see . . . why did I get into that?
The difference between McGrath and me, in that sense, was
that McGrath was fully himself. I wasn't fully myself. I felt that
I needed the Zen training. The haiku had pushed me in that
direction, but there were also other necessities in my life. Some-
thing was missing. I found it in Zen, just as you have found your
life through your aesthetics, perhaps, and through your love of
India. I don't know, would you say so?

GK: *I would say so. I would say my life changed but especially my poetry—once I started practicing meditation and didn't think about it . . . didn't just dabble.*

ACH: Exactly.

GK: *But once I went through the process of inner transformation, it couldn't help but change my poems, because I just thought differently, and I moved and I perceived differently.*

ACH: That's what happened to me. I influenced Prabhasa Dharma Roshi into becoming a poet, as she influenced me into becoming a painter in the time we lived together. She subsequently wrote some fine, fine, poetry. Anyway, we were at the point where McGrath was influential. What else should we say about McGrath?

GK: *Well, I have one follow up, but then I want to move on to Gene and Bert Meyers. How did you see McGrath's profundity on you as a poet? What was it about Tom McGrath as a poet that you felt was significant for you and your development?*

ACH: Prior to my interest in haiku and Zen my interest was political. I was very left-wing, as Tom was, of course. So I admired his work tremendously. That's what formed the friendship—the sense that we shared a common worldview. You know, I met McGrath again in Minnesota years later. He had moved there, to Moorhead [Minnesota State University Moorhead], eventually to the Twin Cities, and so we renewed our friendship.

GK: *What year was that?*

ACH: I went to Minnesota in '75. Later, on McGrath's seventieth birthday, Alice McGrath was there, one of his former wives, and there was a big celebration and we all read poetry. It was a wonderful celebration. Another time, we were at a party and McGrath and my wife (Barbara, my second wife) were dancing together, and he fell and broke his leg!

GK: *Right! I remember that story.*

ACH: I rushed him to emergency. He was in great pain, poor guy. He was a beautiful man. He drank a lot, but what Irishman doesn't?

97

GK: *Speaking of beautiful men . . . our mutual friend Gene Frumkin. One reason we're together as friends is through Gene. Gene always talked to me about you. What was it about Gene's practice as a poet—Gene really gave himself over to the vocation of making a poem—what was it about your relationship with Gene and his work that has been important to you as a poet and an artist?*

ACH: I met Gene when I came back from Ellensburg to L.A., at the time, when Stanley introduced me to McGrath. L.A. was fermenting a type of poetry that was a little different from what San Francisco was doing. They [the L.A. poets] were largely unknown compared to the San Francisco people, but even so, important poets. And, what happened was, I formed a great friendship with Gene. His personality was so attractive that you couldn't help loving the guy. Gene, Mel Weisburd, Stanley Kiesel . . . let's see . . . Keith Gunderson, the Gershgoren brother and sister. A. Fredric Franklyn . . .

GK: *Bert Meyers?*

ACH: No, Bert Meyers was teaching a little distance away, and he was a little more diffident than these guys. These guys wrote a little freer kind of poetry, more Surreal. We formed a group in which we read our poetry once a month—very critically. And that is what, I think, finally helped me find my voice. Gene's to be thanked for that mostly. And Stanley Kiesel. Also, later on, the other poets—a couple of other poets who I mentioned.

GK: *Was William Pillin part of that group?*

ACH: No, he was older. I did know him, and he liked the idea that I was studying Zen. A wonderful, wonderful poet.

GK: *A wonderful poet! He and I share a birthday, obviously not the same year, but we share a birthday. And I have his old kayak [press] books. I have all of his books.*

ACH: Did you meet him?

GK: *I never met him, no. He's one of these people who has just completely fallen off the map.*

ACH: Yes, I know.

GK: *People have no idea who he is.*

ACH: I know. William Pillin was a very delicately formed poet, and a very fine human being.

GK: *And a potter too from what I understand.*

ACH: His wife was a potter. I think he painted the borders or helped in some way. The wife was the potter. And their son is a composer.

GK: *Right. So Gene helped you in terms of his critical awareness.*

ACH: The group helped itself a lot. One time we were running across Hollywood Boulevard—we were talking about forming a group—I think I suggested the title of "The Incognoscenti" so that we could read poetry together as a group and announce our group together. Kiesel thinks he invented the title. I don't know who did, actually.

GK: *And then, you and Gene—*

ACH: We gave a lot of readings together.

GK: *And then you ended up by chance in New Mexico together, an hour-and-a-half or two hours apart, and so your relationship ended up taking on a whole other dimension in your later years, correct?*

ACH: Yeah, what happened was that Gene had a poetry workshop that had initially begun at UCLA. The students had not found the teacher there to their liking, so they found Gene to teach them. Gene, when he was appointed to a position in New Mexico at the University, left the workshop to me. I had never taught, but I said "I'll do it!"

GK: *Oh, I never knew this.*

ACH: Yeah. And so I began to teach poetry, which helped again a lot, because these were very fine poets—Rosella Pace, Ameen Alwan—people who were published already but had wanted more help, so we went on for several years that way. Years later, I came to New Mexico—years, years later—and renewed my friendship with Gene once again. Gene left me that gift, which helped me a lot financially because I was broke. I was poor as a church mouse.

GK: *You mentioned Mel [Weisburd], and obviously we've talked about Gene. Mel has a wonderful poem that you actually read to me once about the three of you in Laurel Canyon during the early days of LSD experiments when it, obviously, was still legal. In fact, Mel, in his memoir, says that prior to Allen Ginsberg [he was] the first to actually describe the LSD experience.*

ACH: I think so.

GK: *Now, he also says somewhere in that unpublished memoir—I think he's calling it* **The Smog Inspector**—*that he noticed after your experimentation with LSD that you moved into a direction of multidisciplinarity. That was one of the factors, in his estimation, that moved you toward a reciprocal alignment in your artistic venture between being a poet and being a painter—and I do want to talk about you as a painter in this interview too . . . we'll get to that—and you as a musical composer. Is that an accurate assessment?*

ACH: Yes, it is, but I have to say this: that it was through Josephine Chuey, who was another poet who had a wonderful, gorgeous house on top of Beverly Hills . . . through her I met this psychiatrist when the drug was still not a street drug (it was still legal) who was experimenting with artists to get their reactions to the drug. So, I took it with this psychiatrist at his office.

GK: *In his office? What year was this?*

ACH: Oh, gosh, I don't remember . . .

GK: *'61, '62 maybe?*

ACH: In the Sixties, yeah. Probably '61 or '62. And the experience was *profound* for me. It showed me I had a . . . what I saw was that what I call an orange personality: that my personality is essentially the color orange.

GK: *Which means what to you?*

ACH: Which means that it freed me to know that I could do many things. That I could paint. I didn't paint until much later, but the beginning of the seeds was there. That the mind could do a number of things. Okay, so then subsequently when I took

LSD again, Gene Frumkin was there to guide me, to be my host in a sense.

GK: *Because he had already done it? He had already experimented with it?*

ACH: No, Gene hadn't yet. No. It happened at the house of Josephine Chuey, because you can see all of L.A. below you. And I took it, and he was just simply there to watch that I didn't fall over the balcony or whatever, and Mel came and saw us later. By then the drug was illegal. Gene took it there, also, another time, and I was guarding him. He sat facing a door, which was . . . these doors of that plywood, that very fine plywood. The shapes in the door were fascinating to him. I remember that! During my "trip," when he left to get some food and came back with Mel, I was left alone for a while. It was sunset time and these clouds were moving over the sky. I put on Mahler's *Das Abschied*, and I was so deeply moved to see the earth moving like that, with the clouds just caressing this earth. It was a fantastic experience. Very heartfelt and very painful in a way. Nostalgic. Anyway, great, great experiences with LSD. So, yeah, it freed me. LSD is a wonderful thing if you get the pure stuff. I don't recommend it for young people because you need to be mature enough to understand what's going on.

GK: *Before you're shattered. Because it shatters your reality.*

ACH: Right, right, it does shatter. Absolutely. You're born again. You have to come back out.

GK: *Now, this was prior to your practice of Zen?*

ACH: Yes.

GK: *So tell me, then, the year and the circumstances—had you started practicing Zen before you met Gisele, or did you both begin to practice it together?*

ACH: No, for me it was something that I had been studying since Ellensburg, since the haiku days. I began to read Alan Watts, Suzuki, a lot of people, and it was all mental. When I met Gisele, we went one day to Josephine Chuey's house and there was this Master there: Sazaki Roshi. So we decided to study Zen, then, the real way, by meditation, which meant six – seven hours a day in spite of the fact that I had a job. It was hard, and after one year I couldn't handle it. Gisele wanted to continue studying very seriously; I couldn't have a job or see my kids on the weekends. It was a disaster for me in a way. So, I left. We broke up.

GK: *But you'd never left the practice.*

ACH: She never left. She went to Japan.

GK: *But, I mean, you never left the practice. You didn't meditate seven hours a day, but you still meditated every day.*

ACH: Yes, but, subsequently, she went to Japan to study. And when she came back she was made a Master by Dr. Thich Man Giac, the highest Buddhist in Vietnam, who was at that time living in Los Angeles. By contrast, Sazaki Roshi hasn't made anybody a Master to this day, and he's over a hundred years old. He was a womanizer and that's the one thing that I disliked the most about him. There were all kinds of troubles there with women. It was not a pretty sight.

GK: *This was the San Francisco Zen Center?*

ACH: No, no, no, no. That's Suzuki. This is Sazaki Roshi.

GK: *Oh, right.*

ACH: A good Master, but a bad human being. And I'm writing a novel based on all that period because I want to present a fact that's very important to Zen—that the practice of Zen has to be pure. If the man is involved with accidental encounters that hurt other people, there's something flawed about that Master, and it should be exposed. Just as you would expose priests who are fooling around with little boys, which is even worse, but that kind of thing. There's something about sex that doesn't mix with religion. Human beings are driven by sex, and then when they want religion they can't separate themselves from the sex, so there's all kinds of problems.

GK: *Yeah, I wonder if one of the problems is the power dynamic. The Master or the Guru has a kind of power but in the sexual encounter—and* *part of what you try to do through meditation or self-realization is to understand your sense of inner power but have that power be a kind of natural flow or fruition where you're not bound or caught by the power— even if you're the victim of such sexual advances, you're still caught in the power dynamic in a really profound way, because you're giving over your power or you're, in a sense, looking for power . . .*

ACH: You know, it's very strange. There are women who are attracted like moths to Masters, and they fall under their sway, and so the Master has to be very pure not to allow it to come to fruition because the woman eventually suffers. It's not that I, as a man, was ever affected by that because he was not gay. It's just with women—I saw many cases of that. Very sad. Very painful to see.

GK: *Did the reverse happen much when there would be a woman Zen Master?*

ACH: Never. With Prabhasa Dharma Roshi . . . when Barbara met her, after she [Prabhasa Dharma] became a Master, Barbara had never liked her too much because she had been with me. Barbara was jealous of our relationship until finally Barbara and I got together. She became a Master and came here, and we both heard this wonderful discussion between Prabhasa Dharma Roshi and a Jewish Rabbi who happens to be an atheist. It was a beautiful discussion between East and West, and we saw that we had to study with her, and I didn't want to do it by myself because we had had a relationship, and I didn't want that to happen. And it never did, afterwards, of course. Barbara felt strongly that she wanted to study with her too, and her first meeting—at a *sesshin*—her first encounter with her as a Master in a *sesshin* in California, Barbara had a very powerful experience. Very powerful. And she's now studying (tonight!) with a teacher who lives nearby who's a woman and a very fine teacher. A *Sensei*. Prabhasa Dharma made a number of us *Sensei*—made me and a few advanced students—teachers [*Sensei*], so we can handle koans or a funeral or a wedding. In other words, we're like priests in a way.

GK: *That's very strange you mentioned that she ordained you as a* Sensei, *because I was going to ask: What did that mean to you? You just described what it means that you can handle koans, but what did that mean personally for your sense of self or no-self? Was that an instrumental moment in your life when you were ordained a* Sensei?

ACH: It's a responsibility. First of all, you have to take the vows, and then the responsibility is that if you have students, you don't abuse them. You've got to help them. I've had two students. That's all. Eventually, I couldn't handle any more physically. I couldn't sit any longer properly, and so I had to tell them good-bye. Because a *Sensei* is really only an *introductory* voice. We are preparing students to really work with a Master. A Master is one who understands so totally that they cannot make a mistake unless they're flawed.

GK: *And what are the vows that you took?*

ACH: Oh, my goodness, I would have to dig them out for you. I don't have memory. You know, I had an accident coming back from a Zen center in Holland after teaching poetry there. We were rear-ended very badly. Subsequently, I had blood in the brain, and they had to operate. I asked the surgeon afterwards about it, and he said, "Yes, when you open the brain to light, and light comes into the brain, you lose memory." So, I don't remember many things. And, the vows, I have them, of course, written down, and I know them by heart—*in* my heart—but not the words.

GK: *Viscerally. They're in your nerve endings.*

ACH: Yes, viscerally.

GK: *Is this the black ice accident in Minneapolis, or is that a different accident?*

ACH: We never had a car accident in the Twin Cities. We had a black ice accident here in New Mexico, coming home one night when we turned over. It didn't harm us.

GK: *There was an accident after which you used the money from the accident to go to Morocco.*

ACH: Oh, yes, that's when we turned over here. They gave us enough money to buy a new car, but then there was extra money. We went to Morocco because I had a powerful dream, which eventually became a novella, but I wanted to see the land so that I could write properly about Morocco. Then we went to Spain and had a wonderful time. That was that accident. The accident in Holland led to this operation.

GK: *I see. Speaking of Morocco, we were in your gallery today—Mary Ann, and Bootsie, and I—and we saw many of your paintings, and we saw you're still continuing with the Moroccan series. I'd like to shift the discussion a little bit to painting now, because we haven't talked a whole lot about painting, and here we are a few feet from the Cardona-Hine Art Gallery. How do you see the relationship—how painting is interconnected with poetry and Zen for you, your Zen practice? We had the honor this evening of listening to your new musical composition as well. So, can you talk a little bit about how these four factors, or more perhaps—Zen, poetry, painting, and musical composition—inhabit one another and feed one another?*

ACH: Okay. I will have to talk a little bit about the three major influences in my life. One is Zen, which has to do with structuring your everyday life. The other is the Castaneda books, which has to do with magic, with the power of the sorcerer, or being a warrior, and the third is, interestingly enough, the Seth Material.

GK: *Oh, really?*

ACH: Yes. The Seth Material is material being given to a woman by a voice from outer space.

GK: *Jane Roberts, I think?*

ACH: Jane Roberts, exactly. The first book of the Seth Material was given to me by a very wonderful human being. She said, "Álvaro, you have to read this." She gave me the book. I looked at it, and I realized that I didn't want to read it. It was, as I said, a voice coming from outer space. Being a Zen person, I didn't want to believe that. But, then, I began to read it because of her power over me. This woman is a very beautiful human being. I'll think of her name in a minute. It's Camille Bertolet. I read it, and the book was *filled* with wisdom, but really an extraterrestrial kind of wisdom. So, I have the voice in me already that speaks for something that is unavoidably optimistic, powerful, eternal; I have the warrior from the Castaneda books, and I have the daily practice through Zen. That allows me to be able to know that in my brain, with my brain, with my mind, I can either paint, write poetry, compose, or do any other thing that I might choose to do, but I haven't because I think that those three are enough. I don't want to be greedy. Remember that I studied music with Stanley Kurnik in L.A. very briefly because I couldn't stand the teaching methods of Americans, so I left. I'm self-taught mostly in both music and painting. Poetry also, as a matter of fact. I'm self-taught in all of those traditions. The possibility that I could do all these things came not only from LSD but from these three sources: Zen, the Seth Material, and Castaneda's Don Juan, the notion that it's possible to use great personal power that's inborn in all of us. It's not that I'm a special kind of person. It's in all of us. You just have to wake up to it, that's all! It's just so simple. But most people have great inhibitions about themselves. They put themselves down. Christianity, for instance, begins with the notion that you are born in sin. That is just plain old bullshit! That is what depresses most human beings to begin with. They believe in it. Most people believe in it consciously or unconsciously that they're not worthy of something. A lot of people come to my gallery and they say, "Oh, I wish I could draw like that or paint like that," and I say, "You could if you just try!" I don't believe in geniuses, by the way. I don't believe there's such a thing. I think we create ourselves in accordance to inner laws. Naturally, there are people born like Mozart with the skills, or like Rimbaud, who we were talking earlier about, who have it from birth. They have *that* knowledge in themselves from birth. Some of us have to work at it and get it, but we *can* get it! You know, that's my belief, anyway. Does that explain something about—

GK: *It does!*

ACH: Well, let me just add one more thing, George. There's no direct connection between music, painting, and poetry. There's no direct connection.

GK: *That's what I was wanting to know more about.*

ACH: It's like being a land with three rivers. Some people have one river, some people have two, some people have three. You can have any number of them.

GK: *You could easily be a basket weaver as a fourth one.*

ACH: Yes, exactly, exactly.

GK: *Since we're on the topic of your paintings, you have hundreds. We looked at many today in your gallery, but you have a special few that you call your mythic paintings, and these began coming to you in the Eighties, I believe, when you were living alone in Minneapolis. What is it about these paintings that you see that makes them mythic or special or somehow different from your other paintings? We even looked at a painting today, and I said "Ah, that looks like one of your mythic paintings," and you said, "Yeah, almost," or "sort of." Right? There's that qualifier. How do you know when one of those paintings is particularly mythic?*

ACH: Let me begin with a small correction. I was not living alone in St. Paul. I was with Barbara.

GK: *Okay.*

ACH: But it didn't begin there. The real painting began there, and I began to sell there, but it was when we were here that the large painting called "Isis" came, and I say "came" because I was working on a large old canvas and trying to get a figure out of it, and all of a sudden I saw that she was not just a figure. She was speaking a different language, and she ultimately became the goddess, Isis, with a very African hairdo, and little arms that are like little wings; the body's twisted around, and it's an awkward painting, but the best painting I've ever done. Why? Because it came from somewhere that was out of control for me, in a way. It was scary for me to paint it because I had never done mythic paintings. I've always been interested in anthropology and this and that, but this, for it to come from me was very mysterious. I took advantage of that kind of energy at that time and made a number of paintings, which were both Egyptian and Buddhist, and those are the mythic paintings that always come. I can't force them. What you saw was forced—I use the word "forced." In other words, I intend to paint something. And that's not mythic. When I see that my intention is to paint something, no matter how nice it may be or how accurate as a painting, how true as a painting, it's still part of me that's earthly. But when a mythic painting comes, it's otherworldly.

GK: *Now, something that just occurred to me—all the years I've known you, I just realized that "mythic" could be understood in a couple of different ways. I've never understood it thematically when you've said this is a mythic painting, but as I heard you talk in the beginning about "Isis," in a sense the content was mythic. It's interesting to me when you have said "mythic painting," I've always considered it mythic energy—that there was something energetic about it. For instance, the painting that I looked at today, I didn't look at it and think, "That looks like a mythic theme. I bet it fits in the series." It had an energy about it, a presence that seemed to be in that moment of letting go you just talked about being sort of scary. It was the painting of three figures. It wasn't stretched yet.*

ACH: Oh, okay.

GK: *The three figures in the murky "George-colors" that we talked about today. Those sort of moody—*

ACH: Oh, yeah, yeah, yeah.

GK: *Now, it felt mythic in energy. I didn't look at that content-wise. This was interesting: when Mary Ann and I met some painters years ago at an artists' colony, we never talked about painting in the ways they were used to. We talked about paintings in terms of their metaphor and in terms of their energy. It's a different kind of training! We approached it as poets and writers.*

Mary Ann Cain: And a couple of them were really insulted, and they didn't really want to talk to us.

ACH: Oh, no *kidding*? Oh, painters are funny that way.

GK: *Yeah, because we talked about the metaphors, and we were unpacking the energy of it. So it just occurred to me as we were talking that our orientation might have been different, that when I said "mythic," I've* *always thought "energy." Not, "Well the Buddha is mythic, and there- fore here are 'The Bodhisattvas.'"*

MAC: I thought the same thing.

ACH: No, that's very good. Very interesting. I think the mythic space goes both ways, don't you?

GK: *I do.*

ACH: That it's a force that comes from out there, if you want to interpret it that way. Maybe it's an ego trip. I don't know.

GK: *Or, a force in there deep within our psyches. We've gone so far in where we've lived the myth.*

ACH: Yeah, maybe so. But, see, if that's the case, then of course the mythic energy can spill into other planes that are, for me, less mythic. "Mythic," for me, implies "connected with major religions" because I have painted the Christ, also. I don't know if I've ever shown you the Christ that I have painted?

GK: *There's one Barbara loves that she sent me a photo of. Christ on the water . . . there's a vaporous Christ.*

ACH: Right, I call it "Seafaring Christ."

GK: *"Seafaring Christ." That's the one I was thinking of. Right. We talked about using it for our book, and then I didn't feel it was right.*

ACH: No, it wasn't. The problem with Jesus is that he's loaded with traditional expectations and notions that damage the actual image of that man, of that creature, as a mythic form. I think that a lot of people see him only as a way to get to heaven.

GK: *Let's talk a little bit about Surrealism. You made a statement earlier that LSD freed you from so much, and there's a favorite Greek Surrealist of mine, Miltos Sachtouris, who lived this Kafkaesque life in an Athens apartment and went to the same butcher every other day down the block and had this small, little physical world but had this immense imagi- native world. He has this great statement. He said, "Surrealism freed me from many things." I think about how Surrealism isn't necessarily a word that carries a lot of positive connotation nowadays because of some of the abuses and excesses—painters like Salvador Dalí, who I deeply* admire, but who became pop-cultural icons. In a way, Surrealism began, in our culture, to become kind of perverted. I don't know if you remember the old Alka-Seltzer commercials?—Dalí was on Alka-Seltzer commercials; he was on "What's My Line?" that old television program.

ACH: He was a scoundrel of the first magnitude, but a great painter. Some of the religious paintings he did of the Christian themes are incredible. Anyway, what you said about this Greek poet reminds me of Bachelard* who used go to the butcher and test the meat—he always checked the meat, the fish, whatever.

GK: I love Bachelard. I didn't know that story!

ACH: And a great imagination, too.

GK: A great imagination. You're not the kind of person to walk around and say, "I'm a this or a that. I'm a Surrealist, I'm a Cubist," and yet, there are certainly elements of Surrealism in your work, and we share poets in common whom we love: César Vallejo, Miguel Hernández, Federico García Lorca, who have all been either influenced by Surrealism or have helped move Surrealism into the direction it became. What is it about Surrealism that has seeped into your poetry and painting, and into your psyche?

ACH: Well, it began with a García Lorca book of poetry entitled **Poet in New York,** which is his most Surrealist work, and I couldn't understand it! I was eighteen years old. Stanley Kurnik had introduced me to him. I couldn't *believe* it. You know, hitting a black man on the head with a spoon . . . and incredible things! But you know what? It just sank like a hook down into the ocean to me and fished me out of the waters of ignorance into a world where everything's possible. You can say anything you want. I see it in you. You are a master Surrealist because you can just say anything in a poem and there it is, my god! You're dredging up the most incredible word combinations, which is fascinating for a poet, you know, to play with language. It frees language. It

---

*Gaston Bachelard (1884-1962), French philosopher whose works on poetics are some of the best, especially **The Poetics of Reverie, The Poetics of Space,** and **Psychoanalysis of Fire**, all available in English.

really frees you. Either be that way, or be a little more restrained sometimes. I like a little restraint sometimes. Certainly in haiku you have to be. Some of the other things that I write, I don't use Surrealism, but there are times when you feel like being wild. It's a wildness! The wildness in us has to find expression one way or another. Traditional forms of art do not allow you to express wildness. You think of more traditional poets, you know, like T.S. Eliot—the **Four Quartets.** I think that's Surreal.

GK: *That's his best poem as far as I'm concerned.*

ACH: Yeah, his best work! Incredible. Magnificent.

GK: *And people ignore that. They talk about "The Wasteland," they talk about "[The Lovesong of J. Alfred] Prufrock," but the* **Four Quartets** *is . . .*

ACH: I know. The **Four Quartets** is it for me too.

GK: *Me too.*

ACH: Well, that's the freedom. He was wild there. Wonderfully wild. So many other poets—Anyway, did I answer your question?

GK: *Yes. The other influence besides Zen, Surrealism, and all of these things we've talked about is certainly the influence of Chinese poetry—*

ACH: Oh, yes.

GK: *. . . on your life and on your work. Without making you feel uncomfortable—I hope I don't make you, inadvertently, feel uncomfortable—my hero in Chinese poetry is Wang Wei, and I've always seen you as kind of a modern-day Wang Wei because Wang Wei was a composer (he played the lute), and he was a master painter—although none of his paintings have survived.*

ACH: But I want to say something that might make you uncomfortable. There's one way to be wrong, and that is to compare me to Wang Wei. (laughter)

GK: *Well, I don't mean it too literally, except as a sign of affection.*

ACH: Thank you!

GK: *Wang Wei was somehow able to bring poetry, music, and painting together. One of the other things about Wang Wei is, although he was a public person, he had to have solitude. He retreated to his hermitage; he spent most of his time hanging around with monks; he wanted the satsang of being with people who "knew." So first I'll put Wang Wei out there, but any other Chinese poets? What has been their impact on you—particularly as a poet and a painter?*

ACH: Well, Tu Fu, and Po Chu-i, I think, and Li Po, of course. There are others whose names I can't even remember that have been so influential because they were saying important things in a simple way. It's amazing. You know that their forms were difficult. When you read a translation, it's a free translation. So that has freed the West to write seriously without having to impose upon ourselves the idea of writing a sonnet or whatever, but the Chinese *did* have that—very tight forms—and yet they were able to say greatly important things, simply.

GK: *Simply, yeah.*

ACH: I love that. Yeah, Wang Wei is really something.

GK: *One of the things that I tell my students to get them to think about Chinese poetry is imagine in the T'ang Dynasty three or four Shakespeares walking around together at the same time: Li Po, Tu Fu, Wang Wei, Po Chu-i. Then they get interested because they tend to think there was a Master, but that was such a high point in Chinese and Asian art.*

ACH: Yeah! It's exactly like Beethoven, Haydn, and Mozart knowing each other. I don't know if they ever all three were together at one time in a tavern or whatever, but they lived at the same time.

GK: *It blows your mind to think about.*

ACH: And then Schubert came just shortly after that. It's amazing!

GK: *You mentioned Stanley Kurnik earlier, and you had an aside. You said one of the things in your eventual separation was that he was more of a traditionalist?*

ACH: Yes, he rhymed everything.

GK: *It was an aesthetic argument that could never be resolved?*

ACH: It led to my dissatisfaction with what he was writing, and I couldn't honestly continue to praise his work, but the thing that ignited the disagreement was that he had put on a play of mine at the First Unitarian Church, and it was very well done and beautiful. He had directed it. It was with some professional actors. Subsequently, I wrote another play, a more serious play, and another fellow named Dwayne-something-or-other was going to direct it. He wanted really professional actors only, and Stanley refused, because I guess maybe he had to pay money, or whatever. Whatever the problem was, the play was not put on, and we felt that Stanley was being too much of an amateur. There was something amateurish about Stanley's approach to art. So that separated us. And it's very unfortunate because I *loved* him. When he was killed by a hit-and-run driver, my first wife called one day and said that Stanley was killed. I was so heartbroken. I wrote a piece of music for him, an elegy. It's never been performed, but there it is. He was a very, very sweet and loving comrade. I'm ready to cry.

GK: *It's good that you can still honor that he helped introduce you to this world of art in such a vital way.*

ACH: He was very vital, very sweet. He should be remembered, not for his art necessarily but for his humanity. Prior to his death, he spent his life helping the blind, teaching the blind poetry and music. And also when he died, somebody in Los Angeles is wearing his eyes, because he had donated his sight to some blind person.

GK: *Since we're talking about the old days, Bert Meyers—you were good friends with Bert.*

ACH: Very good.

GK: *Tell us a little about Bert and that relationship, and the impact that you and Bert had on one another as writers.*

ACH: I first met Bert when I was studying at City College. He

113

was not studying at City College, but he would come around and we would sit in a little café across the street and talk poetry. He was a very handsome man and very well endowed with great talent.

GK: *And brilliant, I understand. He never went on to a higher degree but still had some sort of professorial position.*

ACH: Yes, he was self-taught, and he disciplined himself to write a very fine kind of imagist poem with his images. His images are brilliant. But that led to something peculiar, subsequently, and we were a little distant for a while for several reasons. One was that I and the others, like Gene, felt that he considered himself a little superior to the rest of us because of his skill in writing this kind of poem. Subsequently, he became a teacher at one of the colleges. We continued our friendship and we loved to get together when our kids were small. We wrote haiku back and forth to each other. Very few people know that. He was interested in haiku. But there was always a little edge to the friendship. He was a difficult guy in some ways— beautiful but difficult. He had not much use for free poetry, for Surrealism. He didn't go into that field. He had had emotional problems as a young man. That's why he was not in school at the time. When he found out that I had taken LSD, and that I was influencing Gene in that direction, and Mel, he felt that we were using drugs to help us write our poetry. In other words, he thought we were *leaning* on drugs. Since he couldn't take them, he felt superior and once wrote a poem in which he subtly criticized poets who used other means to get to, presumably, where he was. It was that kind of thing.

GK: *Is that poem in one of his books? Can I look it up?*

ACH: Yes, you can. I'd have to find it for you. That cooled the thing off. Many years later, when he was dying, we got in touch with each other. His wife, Odette, was a wonderful woman. She was a French woman, a Jew who had managed to escape into Switzerland. The rest of the family, I guess, had gotten killed. Beautiful person. She was great. She called me on the phone and thanked me so strongly that I had come back into Bert's life. I had reviewed the book that he had published just before he died, gave him a good review, and he was very happy with that. So, we again made up.

GK: *Full circle.*

ACH: Yeah, full circle.

GK: *That's beautiful. Now, you were talking about your kids, and I saw old pictures—of when they did that special* **St. Elizabeth Street** *Issue on Gene—of Gene with the pipe and the baseball bat at Griffith Park?*

ACH: I've never seen that.

GK: *Oh, that's a great photo! Are these the Griffith Park softball games you're talking about with the families?*

ACH: No, we would meet in other parks with the little kids playing around. We would have a picnic. We never played baseball together.

GK: *Okay. Gene's got this ubiquitous pipe and he's got the bat, and he's swinging it.*

ACH: Subsequently, he went into smoking little cigars, and then he had to give it up.

GK: *One more interesting thing about Gene, and then I want to talk about what's happening with your recent work. I wanted to mention that when Gene visited several years ago, I had that old issue of* **Bachy** *[the L.A. literary magazine] when Bert had just died, and I showed it to you when you visited as well. I'll never forget—Gene sat in a chair and opened it. It was the Special Issue on Bert Meyers, and he said, "Ahh, Bert Meyers." It was this quality in his voice of deep affection and longing—*

ACH: Well, everybody respected him.

GK: *. . . to just see his friend's photo and to see an issue on Bert Meyers. I was very touched by that.*

ACH: Gene never had a bad word about anybody. He was a saint.

GK: *He was a saint, yes. You're 83 years old, about to turn 84, Columbus*

Day if I recall, right?

ACH: Yes.

GK: *Where do you see your work going now in this phase of your life? I know you're pulling together some interesting poetry manuscripts; you just had this musical composition performed in Grand Rapids; you're painting up a storm. You're still doing all this. What can you tell us about the recent work and where you see yourself in this phase of your life?*

ACH: One of the most important things that has happened to me lately is meeting you and collaborating in that book we wrote. What was the title?

GK: *(chuckles)* **The Recumbent Galaxy.**

ACH: The Recumbent Galaxy. And your great warmth and love for my painting—that's moved me a great deal. It has made me feel very, very good and very wanted. So, it has opened up that Surrealist vein again, because that book is fairly surreal. I'm now considering writing a book called **Antiphons for Gödel and Einstein** where I would quote Gödel and Einstein about time and about the universe, and then write my poems in between as antiphons.

GK: *I love it!*

ACH: It's really, I think, an echo of my knowing you that has allowed me to want to move in different directions.

GK: *Really?*

ACH: Yeah. I'm still working on several other manuscripts. One is called **Zen On the Way to Die,** which is an account of all the people I've known who have died, and how they died, and how it is a Zen way to die no matter how you die. That's a Zen way.

GK: *Zen AND the Way to Die, or Zen ON the Way to Die?*

ACH: ON the Way to Die. It has a double meaning. Another manuscript I'm working on is **Phantom Buddha,** which is a novel based on Gisele and me and the troubles we had with Sazaki Roshi. What else? I even forget. I have a desire to write two symphonies. One is a choral symphony with poems by Vallejo, Lorca, and my brother Alfredo. And then, another symphony, which is going to be mythical—I mean, not mythical. What is the word I want? Well, I envision it musically. I haven't got words for it. It's incredibly . . . ethereal. That's what I wanted. Right now I'm working on a couple of things. I'm orchestrating some songs—the songs of Synge, J.M. Synge—which I had written for a small group of instruments, but I'm orchestrating them for full orchestra. I'm also halfway through an opera. You know, it's crazy-making, because at my age I should be concentrating on a little tiny thing like writing more haiku, but instead it's all over the place!

GK: *Well, the theme of what we talked about earlier was that you were freed to realize you could move in many directions. It seems like you're just following those streams to their logical continuation.*

ACH: Yeah, but the streams are opening into deltas, and they're mixing up their waters, and it's just kind of weird.

GK: *Well, one of the things I really love about you is that you don't just construct yourself in limiting terms like "I'm the poet," or "I'm the artist." I want to talk about family life—to close this interview off—and animals. We've spent the afternoon with your two bulldogs, Chocho and Tula, and with your wife Barbara . . .*

ACH: And your little dog.

GK: *And our little dog, Bootsie, and Mary Ann. Barbara is also a painter and poet. Could you say a few things about your relationship with Barbara as collaborators, in a sense, living in the same house, getting up and both practicing Zen, both writing poetry, both painting—and your relationship with your animals? Not only do we have the two bulldogs here, but in the backyard we have three of your four previous bulldogs buried in a sacred triangle at the top of the mountain here.*

MAC: And Gaia.

ACH: And the cat.

GK: *And the cat, Gaia, walking around. I guess this is a question about domesticity. Can you say a little about your relationship with your wife,* *your relationship with animals, and how that feeds your psyche?*

ACH: Well, we are at a point in life when we value little things—the daily occurrences—and they're buttressed by animals who adore you. That is a wonderful thing to have, I think. We were lucky to discover that. The first bulldog we got was Machita in St. Paul, Minnesota. I had wanted a bulldog. I had the wrong notion that in the old movies I had seen as a child of "Our Gang"—that that was a bulldog. Actually, it was, I think, a Boston Terrier. But I had the notion of a bulldog. So we went and found this darling little baby bulldog, we brought this little bulldog home, and we fell madly in love with her and she with us. That was the beginning of that. That's domesticity at its best, I think.

The other thing is to be careful in relationships so that you don't rub each other wrong. I am, in spite of what you may think about me, very irritable. I flare up very easily. I have to control that very much because when you're living with another human being, no matter how close they are to you, or how much like you they are in terms of ideas or art or whatever, there's always something that they do that irritates you and vice versa. We're very careful with that, so that we respect each other. Respect is essential to a long-lasting relationship. She's a very forgiving woman. I value her very highly. She's probably the only woman in the world who I could possibly have an existence with.

GK: *Anything else we didn't cover that you feel like you'd like to say?*

ACH: We've covered everything except my birth and my death!

GK: *Well, we don't have to worry about your death because you're going to be with us for many, many years.*

ACH: (laughter) I want to thank you very, very much from the bottom of my heart for who you are and what you're doing for me.

GK: *It's my honor.*

ACH: You and your wife are exemplary human beings. Beautiful.

Words Again

The water of language
boils in the skull
I brew a tea of words
and serve it from my mouth

A cup at a time
burning my lips
perhaps a lonely horse
in its maze of green.

Hermitage

Old age
will be a mountain
deep
among pines

the silence will be a flute
the wind can lean on

Putting Your Shadow
on Backwards

(A memory of Taos pueblo)

The brook cuts
right through the village

If you want bread
they have it on either shore.

119

Haiku from
The Gathering Wave

Spring

Looking at the moon
suddenly remembering
to look at the moon.

The moonlight involved
in the paleness of the rose
darkens the cypress.

This is the season
when chrysanthemums return
your gift of water.

It rains how it rains
birds of the mountain cower
in a few places.

The moss-covered rock
on either side endlessly
much endless water.

You and your life and
all the clean clothes of my heart
waving in the breeze.

The plum tree in bloom
five thousand miles of childhood
veiled at its wedding.

You hear frogs like that
in bucket after bucket
of utter darkness.

Only a cricket knows
how to saw the night in half
half rooster   half star.

Summer

The summer orchard
a turtledove calls softly
from its green tunnels.

Caressing at once
both bull and black horizon
the summer lightning.

The swollen river
drowns out the afternoon's raid
of his loquat trees.

The fork in the road
precipitated by this
chirimoya tree.

She can no longer
keep her two feet on the ground
ringing that school bell.

Forcing the bamboo
to throw them in the water
the naked schoolboys.

The gathering wave
sand-pipers venturing in
among the children.

Her golden urine
all over the squash flowers
the runaway goat.

Mushrooms and ladies
dangerous varieties
are beautiful too.

Peeling tangerines
somehow all that I care for
here in the fragrance.

The sail is so black
and the leaf so very green
that the bloom is red

Autumn

I hear the crickets
but if the wind were to change
I'd sit in darkness.

The moon in the sky
still the dandelion
lands in the water.

The white rooster dreams
that the loveliest hen of all
is out of his reach.

The cry of the bird
plunges into the water
for an endless drink.

I don't know the wind
if it carries more for laughter
or for oblivion.

The old woman died
in her proud little garden
lettuce goes to seed.

The grave digger blinks
high winds carry the spider
over the ocean.

Daytime flowers here
come I'll race you down the hill
nighttime flowers there.

I hug the children
and one in the bunch laughs out
hearing my heart beat.

The village idiot
on the crests of the cypress
she's missed her supper.

The cold blackberries
hung just above the water
oh, the swift river.

My grandmother's tomb
on a day of small white clouds
and eternity.

Winter

Fog introducing
the grizzly bear to the stag
in an even voice.

His very first snow
our cat stock-still in the yard
arranging his thoughts.

The snow patiently
and the wind a slight tug
conversing with me.

Poinsettias and wind
and a wall and the night of
wind and poinsettias.

Goya

Goya escape por ésta vez del Aqueronte avaro;
está muy arrogantillo, y pinta que se las pela,
sin querer corregir jamás nada de 10 que pinta

Goya has escaped this time from miserly Acheron;
he's been feeling mighty smug, and painting like all get-out,
without looking to correct ever anything he does ...
- from a letter by Moratín to Juan Melón, 1825

he threw himself into the silver-squandered waters
the dark design hounded by the task of lead
that slowly poisoned his life
just as the scrupulous world was left behind
and fresh orders of pain stripped
his conventional skin

he heard his own daemonic scream
in the pit of eternity heard it
against the tender blue delphinium colors
he was used to using oh
when he was young he began prettily
on loose canvasses he caught Court beauties
hiding behind fans
then came the havoc of the French
flesh ripped off flesh
the sun never to shine again

in his *El Gran Cabrón* a painting
longer than the rooms where the police have sanction
a small girl faces Satan across a sea of witches
the huge horned beast stares directly at her
and she perhaps ten seated on a household
chair she doesn't flinch
curiosity will have those two

look into each other for all time
while the centuries herd us from luck
to formal slaughter
for this is a work where the valves
of the heart lie exposed a heartbeat away
from the next disaster

Mussorgsky Drunk

in the famous portrait by Shchukin
one sees the bloated face
the bloodshot eyes
the bulbous nose

the end cannot be far
a lifetime in dingy rooms
empty bottles all around
peeling wallpaper
ink on his fingers
broken-down pianos

and a music as from some deep well
in the heart of Russia

a lot of things with time
must have climbed the spidery
sunflower of his childhood

they never clogged the throat
of the caged bird in the swaying birch

Segovia

to Carmen Candela

I asked my friend why she had brought us here
what we saw on entering was disappointing
an industrial order so barely human
nobody could be seen the desolate buildings
proud to be cold a hint of the Spain
I would never have visited

we descended a ravine between barren hills
and then as a wonder the Roman aqueduct
was there skinny and poised like my father
stone upon stone till very high above a few VWs

we descended further
spring gardens were celebrating communion
while St. John of the Cross
slept in the chapel

a nightingale prefers to be buried in such a hollow
to join the city one climbs to its horizon
and its pride the alcazar
turreted and intricate as a kaleidoscope
home to dragon slayers in the morning sun
of a medieval and impossible faith

Listen Galaxea

Galaxea
be kind to Galileo Galilei
who is thrust upon you
in the extremity of his need
grant him permission to poke around
he imagines he investigates
and I love him dearly dearly
he is almost blind
but who needs eyes
when they have you Galaxea
in whose embrace webs of eternity
rock gently to and fro
take this man Galaxea
to be your lawful wedded mite
and see that you nurture him
and provide for his sustenance
guarding him from the violence
of your real lovers the gods
in whose arms you burst
like a bubble of joy
ah Galaxea Galaxea
to think that it was your own little whim
to invent him this man
what was it?
that you couldn't look with your own eyes
at your armpit?
you couldn't see your own beautiful back
graceful as a beach
and you wanted someone to walk
its lovely loneliness a while?
a while only?
listen Galaxea
let me
let him caress you

let our lives fall upon your skin
like a prolonged caress
Galaxea Galaxea
this is a man
with a day's beard behind him talking
let him caress you
while someone awakens
the sleeping horses
Galaxea
I have used one of your days
to comb the beach
for the hymen of doors
it is dark now
I know that Galileo will stumble across
marvelous things in that same dark
which is the milk of Galaxea
Galaxea
if it is within your reach
protect him now that you've made him
pollen man
dandelion man is among you
he is little people
in the eyelash of oblivion
oh Galaxea
see to it that he lives
that he doesn't lapse into despair
that he doesn't sink into stone
that he doesn't faint into thin air
because Galaxea
Galaxa are you listening?
you have no one else smaller than you
to love you
and there is no one else
at the dark beach of your back
running like the wild surf with his lungs
and his now awakened horses

131

Álvaro Cardona-Hine
Basic Bibliography

Romance de Agapito Cascante, (Repertorio Americano, Costa Rica, 1955)

The Gathering Wave, (Alan Swallow, Denver, 1961)

The Flesh of Utopia, (Alan Swallow, Denver, 1964)

Menashtash, (Little Square Book Review, Santa Barbara, 1969)

Agapito, (Charles Scribners' Sons, New York, 1969)

Spain, Let This Cup Pass From Me, (Cesar Vallejo translations, Red Hill Press, 1972)

Words on Paper, (Red Hill Press, Los Angeles, 1974)

Two Elegies, (Red Hill Press, Los Angeles, 1976)

The Half-Eaten Angel (Nodin Press, Minneapolis, 1981)

When I Was a Father, (New Rivers Press, Saint Paul, 1982)

Miss O'Keeffe, (collaboration; University of New Mexico Press, Albuquerque, 1992)

Four Poems About Sparrows, (Eyelight Press, Cordoba, 1994)

A Garden of Sound, (Pemmican Press, Washington, 1996)

A History of Light, (Sherman Asher Publishing, Santa Fe, 1997)

Thirteen Tangos for Stravinsky, (prose memoir; Sherman Asher Publishing, Santa Fe, 1999)

The Curvature of the Earth, (collaboration with Gene Frumkin; Albuquerque, UNM Press, 2007)

The Recumbent Galaxy (collaboration with George Kalamaras; Chattanooga, TN, C & R Press, 2010)

Recent Poetry Volumes in Spanish:

Sucursal de Estrella (Madrid, Ed. Catriel, 2006 & Albuquerque, UNM Press)

Claridades (Madrid, Ed. Catriel, 2007)

Holly Prado

Lunar

I should be washing my face,
flossing my teeth, being a good citizen,
which I have been all day I loved my neighbor
not quite as myself but as closely as I could manage
in the differences between our languages,
our clothes, our families, our ideas of god –

god, god, god and goddess, whom I pray to: please bless
those I care for, especially, today, the young woman
who doubts she has anything

valuable to say.

dear young woman: you are thrilling
in your generous fertility, your social outrage.
let yourself have the brilliantly extreme language you deserve;
let yourself be our shocking medicine, stringent
as the wild tree it springs from.

this sorry world: a little girl in Macy's yesterday:
four years old — jabber, jabber —
floppy pink shorts too too short.
my last glimpse: she sat, trying on way-too-large
strappy, purple sandals with five inch heels.

so, I can't love our girly inheritance — its self-betrayal,
its fractured hips I want Moonhood, woman an owl
who claws her branch, toes meant only for this.

Holly Prado
Shoulders

low level sorrow coming after
dinner when I have nothing left to do
except wonder what will happen in the novel
I'm reading which does matter even if it's

fiction as all our lives are pure imagination —
and then, too, actual as sudden radical Muslim attacks
in Africa kill people watching the World Cup:
blood spilled against simple enthusiasm.

oh, god, our unstoppable revenge.

I read now a young, suicidal man this novel my summer
choice this much recommended book makes me
desperate for solace which my husband offers as he says,
"sometimes it's enough to stand at the open window."

when I fall asleep tonight I'll be wearing cotton drawstring
pants that have shrunk so they don't fit my husband anymore;
he bequeaths these soft, often-washed garments to me,
and I wear them with old t-shirts unglamorous but we've come
to that time in ourselves when it doesn't matter whose
clothes are on our sweet achy bodies. we are all human,

wormy, grumpy, ignoble creatures who still can wish
for angelic presence rescue or annunciation anything
larger than this crappy inheritance of fiction and reality in
        which
anybody can kill anybody even himself does killing solve
a Great Religious Problem, ever? nothing solves us

but grace. how much of that is around tonight?

Gene Frumkin:
A Personal Remembrance and Homage

When you think about the best poets of New Mexico in recent years, names at the top of the list include Keith Wilson and Gene Frumkin. From a personal standpoint, I recall meeting both poets (and Pat Smith) in 1970, the year I moved to this state from Kansas to teach in the Spanish section of what was then the Modern Languages Department at the University of New Mexico. They were not only good writers but personable and congenial to someone new to the state as I was.

My specialty within the UNM Spanish faculty was Hispanic poetry, particularly Latin American poetry, but I was also writing my own poetry in English. I had written and published poetry while I was teaching at the University of Kansas and began publishing some poems in local literary magazines in Lawrence. This led me to attend many readings sponsored by the English Department. In academia, too often, faculty and students in one department have little contact with other departments. However, because of my writing and publishing efforts in Kansas, I didn't fit this profile. For this reason, while at KU, I got to hear, meet, and know the poetry of such poets as Ed Dorn, Robert Bly, Denise Levertov, Robert Creeley, Bob Duncan, Bill Merwin, David Ignatow, Diane Wakoski, Vic Contoski, Jerome Rothenberg, David Antin, Armand Schwerner, Richard Wilbur, Michael McClure, Gary Snyder, and many others. It was a great opportunity to hear these writers, made possible because at that time (late 60s) there was money available and a Chairman willing to spend it on poets.

When I arrived at UNM, however, there were no such budget to bring in big name writers, although a literary guest would come along once in a while. The compensation was that, even then, there was poetry activity in the state and in Albuquerque, which today has grown into a vibrant poetry scene. Poets such as Gene, Pat, and Keith laid the groundwork for the present explosion of poetry activity across New Mexico. And other writers too, like Sabine Ulibarri, Rodolfo Anaya, Simon Ortiz. They fostered an entire generation of excellent poets that are part of the ladder to the current poetic hyper-activity in the state. I do remember a reading in which I participated with Gene, Simon, and others; for me it was an honor to read with them.

After many years in Los Angeles where I taught at USC and UCLA (visiting at UCSD), I returned to New Mexico where I had always planned to retire, and again met up with Gene, Pat, and Keith. Gene was busy with poetry as always, stanzas stacked in corners of his brain, and he came up to the Duende Poetry Series readings in Placitas (begun in 2004), from time to time. Ultimately, it was at that venue, at the Anasazi Fields Winery, where, after his passing, a three-hour tribute reading was held (though not as part of the Duende Series). Attendees, including his family, came in from all over the U.S. And the venue was packed! It was an incredible reading! Gene was honored by New Mexico's poets who gave him a good-bye woven from their words into a poetic vehicle that will carry his memory into the future for all of us who were there, for all of us who read, to remind all of us of Gene's legacy, his many students and especially, his own words.   —GLB

Gene Frumkin: A Basic Bibliography

The Hawk and the Lizard (Denver: Swallow Press, 1963)

The Orange Tree (Chicago: Cyfoeth, 1965)

The Rainbow-Walker (Albuquerque, NM: Grasshopper Press, 1968)

Dostoevsky and Other Nature Poems (San Luis Obispo, CA: Solo Press, 1972)

Locust Cry: Poems 1958-1965 (Albuquerque, NM: San Marcos Press, 1973)

The Indian Rio Grande: Recent Poems from 3 Cultures (co-editor, with Stanley Noyes; Albuquerque, NM: San Marcos Press, 1977)

The Mystic Writing-Pad (Los Angeles: Red Hill Press, 1977)

Loops (Albuquerque, NM: San Marcos Press, 1979)

Clouds and Red Earth (Chicago: Swallow Press, 1981)

A Lover's Quarrel with America (Albuquerque, NM: Automatic Press, 1985)

A Sweetness in the Air (San Luis Obispo, CA: Solo Press, 1987)

Comma in the Ear (Albuquerque, NM: Living Batch Press, 1990)

Saturn Is Mostly Weather: Selected and Uncollected Poems (El Paso, TX: Cinco Puntos Press, 1992)

The Old Man Who Swam Away and Left Only His Wet Feet (Albuquerque, NM: La Alameda Press, 1998)

Falling Into Meditation (Instress, 1999)

Freud by Other Means (Albuquerque, NM: La Alameda Press, 2003)

The Curvature of the Earth (co-author, with Álvaro Cardona-Hine; Albuquerque, NM: University of New Mexico Press, 2007)

Meditations in Crowded Air (Tucson, AZ: Chax, forthcoming)

Escalator

The escalator
is a dangerous enemy
who could trip you
        one step at a time.
This is how the mind works,
synthesizing dream with substance.
      Or as Jung
      alternates
       with Freud.
    The substitution
of ground for holiness
claims voice as a reason
for old tribes locating
the sun
        as figures
in the act, at the window.

The future derives
from sleep, evolves into gods
and animals.
    This is a process
    that F. chilled into
    vin tage prose.
      Jungwarmed
to the blooded world,
not alone. The human collective
    describes the enormity
of a single voice. How the
        minotaur
      poses like God
in his mystical cellar.

    Yet F. too brings the good news
    that deciphers time

in focus, traveled by a map,
      as if one could say
      there it is! now is as good
      as anywhere.
Everything is abstract
      in its origin
     almost
as if Plato
believed in the verity
of his good republic.

The escalator goes flat by
      steps. It continues
      as breath does:
        two men in blue suits with vests.
The moving sidewalk is
       no less.
It slows into watchword, and if F.
      abhorred the occult,
      Jung compared sexuality
   in the psychic order
to a hidden grammar,
      dogma on the harpsichord.

     Organized
     mystery, lens-defined
     hyperbole.
A science rises from obsession,
shaped like the Golem of Prague,
but who remembers
     his song?
Jung catches flies
       instead
       of fish.

F. hangs his briefs
        on the line.
The world is all
  alone,
       all there is
      to imitate.
Time limps behind
the escalator, F. stands
with a stopwatch,
Jung with a camera.
Mind in slow motion, caught in breath.

Narrative of Conscience

A breeze blows through my worksheets
    at five o'clock, when the sun,
        in its decline,
      opens out
to the owl
of the local universe. I have
          followed
       my feet
     through the turnstile
     of this time,
    last night's kitchen a dream
    where I strayed barefoot,
    crawling,
       not knowing
      this was a phase,
only excess of being.

Lithe forms of women slant my mind
to wayward afternoons
      when in youth
    I took purchase
     on punishment,
    There is always
too much to think of How could
       anyone
     rise on the shoulders
   of reverie
to see down below a scarred winter?

Freud was only a

         n
         a
         m
         e

in the crackerjack box.
Later, he slept in me, I, crank
of masturbation,
early riser
    to a girl's breath
      in my mouth,
comrade to beasts, siphoned
            from liquid books.
    Writing is too narrow:
a world glimpsed as a formal
          target.
    I aimed low at Freud,
    crawling on all fours,
    under the table, wax
fruits upon it.

Old now, I read
poetry, and write
for my heart's flickering.
    Old Yeats, be my darkness,
beam through me a glow
    of your Byzantine
    years.
    If in language there could be
reward for lines
      silent in meaning
    yet above mere duty,
I would speak to Auden's
      limestone.
    Song, though old-fashioned,
remains the lodestar,
from back then when syn tax
      refused the noose.

The third millennium:
before it dawns in 24
circles, spaces already its
                numbers
through asteroids' perilous design.
I call for mother, too dead
to believe me. But then she was
                a bastion,
        protector of my childhood,
        adolescence, young manhood.
In my new age I try to wipe
her blue eyes from
                my fingers.
Freud, help me
                sing
        one or two of your great
        oneiric sex-songs.

    I sell my dreams now
for pennies by the pound.
                It's not too late
        to believe
            in Jung's
    collective irony. I too
am a myth, as described in prologues.
Walking the labyrinth is an ancient
spiritual
                exercise.
        I have walked it
on filmy shoes to scan
its negative. My penis
                wakes
                up.
        I think it wants to shout.

I might have been a Language poet,
      but of course
   my tongue is too long.
Instead, I
  respect
   those who crack each word
   with a mallet until it cries
   with joy.
   I am the narrative
of my conscience: I hold the hand
     of strong masters.
  I am pitch black, though
a light swivels through my head.
Yes, old fellow, I talk to myself
       in brackets.
  The main story idles
  in lemon-light.
Nowhere to go but here,
where I eat oatmeal, mango, Cornish hen,
  and pull along the shy God
of my heirs.

Whatsaid Gene:
New poems, new book

In the coming year, Chax Press in Tucson will publish Gene Frumkin's **Meditations in Crowded Air**, poems for the most part inspired by (or, as Gene puts it at the close of many of the poems, "with a debt to") the works of modernist and postwar European and American artists. Comprising forty-nine poems and nearly two hundred pages, it will be Gene's largest collection, but only a hint at the wealth of his unpublished work.

For an epistolary interview conducted in 2003 by poet and close friend Todd Moore, Gene writes:

> *I have now a style that seems to be one I can and want to use in different ways. That is, I work in terms of series. I hope I am redefining myself in terms of these series. I don't want to get stuck in a mood of self-satisfaction that leads to a stiffening of the poetic muscles.*

In this serial method typical of his later work (exemplified by such books as **Comma in the Ear** and **Freud by Other Means**), Gene proceeds through the poem, and from poem to poem, by associative links and disjunctive leaps, mapping areas of thought, feeling, memory, history, and fantasy by moving through them intuitively and musically.

Meditations, ruminations . . . and imaginings. The poems in **Meditations** are fantasias on their subjects rather than simple readings or analyses. Though most are prompted by individual artworks, some repond more generally to one (or more) artist's work and life, and a few have origins in concerns other than art, finding their place in the book by an affinity of style and preoccupation. The series itself is flexible, permeable, nonsystematic.

145

The initial query manuscript mailed to Charles Alexander at Chax contained eighteen poems, five of which were dropped from the next, much expanded, version. Gene continued to add poems to the book over several years, seemingly experimenting with longer and shorter versions of a possible table of contents. In editing the manuscript for publication, I've maintained those features of Gene's organization that persisted through multiple versions, while simultaneously taking the most expansive view of the series that I could justify. The latest of Gene's compilations, found in a file on his computer but never sent, added yet another poem to the book. I'm certain that there would have been more.

– David Abel

Note: With Gene's poems that follow, you may wish to look online at artworks that inspired them. Search for the name of the artwork, or artist; they are all available to see.

"Back Seat Dodge '38, 1964" refers to the controversial Edward Kienholz mixed-media sculpture.

"Blue Horse" references paintings by Franz Marc: see Wikipedia or http://www.artchive.com/artchive/M/marc/blue_horse.jpg.html .

For the poem "Crowded Air," put into the subject line "A star caresses the breast of a negress" and it will bring up websites with the painting of that name by Joan Miró.

"In Memoriam 9/11" has no art references.

"That Civil War in Spain" refers to Francisco Goya's series of drawings and etchings entitled "Disasters of War," and Robert Motherwell's painting series "Elegy to the Spanish Republic."

Excerpts from **Meditations in Crowded Air**

Back Seat Dodge '38, 1964

with a debt to Edward Kienholz

Wasting good money
                          on bad hands,
                    I hold onto
          such images
          as can't be realized.
Such as myself
          in the back seat
                          of that truncated
                                    Dodge,
          a woman's fishnet leg
                          protruding.
Beer bottles on the ground
                    litter this success
                                    story.

                    Creating its web,
          the spider moaned in its
                                    corner
                    of the back seat
where I could hear myself
                          as an echo.
          But were we alive back then
          in the sixties when I heard
          nothing so unlikely
                    as people
discussing us locked
                    in the bloody crackup
                          in the L.A. County
                                    Museum?

          This is now,
          which is always the case.
          This is still a tense
                                    mood,

147

just before the head-on pickup
scattered us like pigeons.
                    As a wage for love,
                         that divine

                                   sensuality,

          cage in which we lie,
one leg extending outward.

          It's a perfect day,
the claw that was then
sticks in my groin. I can
                    barely move
               without her beauty
          rising red in my skin.
          Even if she was
                    stuffed with straw,
I could not look away
or stay clear of that blue

                                   Dodge.
          I go back to the museum,
                    but she has been
stored away until the next

                                   retrospective.

          And where is the blood
               on the carpeting?
We were coming back
               from Santa Barbara,
          the night
was foggy. The pickup
          headed straight into us.
          No one was driving.
                    You screamed, afraid
                         your straw might
                              catch fire.
               A coastal breeze
                    came up,
                         billowing
          the fire.
Afterwards, they cleaned us up.

Blue Horse

with a debt to Franz Marc

Inside the wooden merchant
a truck pulls up, and several horses
prance out onto the weeds where

                rugby

     should have been. The field
is muddy from the rain.
     Other duties call. Certain
occasions defy their own

               directions.

        The wooden merchant
           is not accurate
but vindictive.

        Consecutive logic
does not rein in the specific

              blue horse

     that gallops across the city
to the campus where the professors
     are caressing many fawns and

              elk.

        The wooden merchant
     stands where he always
     stood, in front of the
            cigar store.
The blue horse stamps the ground.

Four foxes gather outside the line
below the white castle high on
          the dark green

              rock.

      A girl in orange
     plays a clarinet in the gathering
at high dusk. My painterly eye
       tempts me into scenes
       that barely take place.
The blue horse is someone

                                              I know
from a previous stampede.

Brisk trading fills the morning hours
                    when the herd
                    is awake to
                          the chill air.
              Bison in Europe? The campus,
gray buildings, pointing to heaven,
much like the castle. The blue
                  horse, walking
                    slowly, almost human,
            pokes his long, handsome

                                              face
at the blond baby and nickers.

The gray monkey on the limb
                peers at a noise
                    behind him,
              or a fraction
of a noise. The professors huddle
            behind the gym, comparing
              aesthetic insults about

                                      animals.
They are low key. This is a new

                                    market
            for them. They feel
they need professional help.

             The wooden merchant,
once the horses were released,
                      has not stirred.
                The blond baby

                                    squalls,
          its mother and father
not to be seen, while the tiger
observes from a small section of

                                  the jungle.
What is needed is perception.

I can't help. I am usually

            surprised

at how little I absorb in any scene,
but I can't forget the blue horse
        that, evidently,
              has been stunned
              by the morning's

            events.

     The other horses wander about
among the spectators.
Have the police been contacted?
        I think about
   a danger that might be
      describing itself
        in some people's minds.
Some are looking for a place
     on the floor
        of tall buildings.

The four foxes might be

            premature

     in their hunt
for a new homeland where
chickens fly to them. As the water
         pauses in a trickle,
    the mood turns darker,
    even among the deer
       in a monastery garden.
         A naked woman
  stoops to wash her feet.
Behind her, revolutionary forces
       march forward
      into the net.

           Havoc

   is the leader's name. He
   misjudged the odds.

Crowded Air

Miró, in the crowded air,
          could seem
one of his shapes: black-rain

                                        crescents,
glowing fish, white eyes coasting
                    in a green medium.
                    So the painter

                                        chooses
          comic stances that become
rituals in a stony-eyed system.
                    What paint can do
                    is to unlock the poem
                    that crawls from its cavern
one syllable at a time.

Reality, then, searches for

                                        wisdom,
                    an orange hand
          tries to capture
          one of the gray fedoras,
with black bands floating easily
                    in the light wind.
No one back then thought
in consecutive epigrams, fortunate
to be alive as a raisin in the

                              carrot cake.
          Miró's hours never ended.
          It might take him
                    years
to juggle lozenges in air.

          But art is only
          a passage from sequel
          to pressures of language
as wild oxygen to innumerable
                    consequent blocks.
          What is at risk
                    can only be arranged

by scholarly quota.
Knock on wood betrays a concern
                    for the real

                                        continuation

                    as abstract focus
and variable hope.

          Texture results from
an addiction to stars in snail

                                        sexes.

We learn that the heart
                    is fragmentary,
                    part reasonable, part

                                        surreal.

               Whatever is wonder
     survives its act
to supervene constructs too

                                        tight

                    to keep the cargo
                    within the range
          of magnetic forces
                    without premeditation.

                         Then one thinks
          of thinking about the star
that caresses the "Breast
                    of a Black

                                        Woman."

          Miró's enigmas
          establish one sort of

                                        certainty:

the mind is a corner
          of imagination
          where the open
falls like spark
          into human resource:
                    the gardens of China.

               Abbreviation
     acts in the flesh

as a tattoo band around a woman's
                                    ankle.
                Miró's band
                        articulates
            a vision of colors
that circle about the primed canvas
            in a primal
                    language viewed
            as location in space.
Art goes only so far among figures
who taste the Milky Way's
                                    fruits
                        and spices,
and there the motion distills itself.

A stranger opens the locked door,
comes into the kitchen
                where the farmer's wife
                                    whimpers,
                holds a golden pail
            that looks like
the horn of plenty. An indifferent
                                    cat
            has watched him enter
the crimson heart's song, more
                                    a valentine
                below the half moon
            than a threat.
This questionable man is made,
                        realistically,
                                    of paper.
                The moment itself
                is a collage,
repeatedly changing places with
                    another desire.
Justice, even in riddles, flies
                    on crude wings
toward the man's kindly, papery
                                    intent.

In Memoriam 9/11

So far from true
it could be envisioned
in helium, and so too
the sunlight stretched between
two tall buildings. In the
falling
a wound opened
for the unwinding of a serpent
offering a poisoned apple,
as everybody watched.
A serene breeze
blew away,
like a caress,
all that remained
in the thin conscience
of death.

The local crumble
of the instant, the time it
took
for the air to rise
above smoking elevators
was enough to create
a nanosecond model of the first
breath
ever taken,
lodged in the soil
of what was yet to be,
a look so Earthly
among the planets
that millennia were to roll before
a word could recognize
a word.

In all that, to establish

a figure of people running
as if from their bodies,
                    the sound
            is for the effect
                of a rehearsal
for Earth's own Big Bang.
Blood does not economize in this

                                    staging.

                It runs through
                the district
            in perfect tune
with death and the dismembering
                    by unique
                        violation.

Sleep will come in a corner
                beside a twisted tree.
                The memory
                of a face
                    on a poster will
                                linger
                as a true dream,
a likeness of who was away
                    in mystic ads,
            in brand new wildflowers.
Traffic strayed into thick streets

                                    of garbage,
                the signals going on
                    but mostly off.
            The subway on its last leg.

            The air was stuffed
        with transitional space,
afforded by a weakening break,

                                    puffs

            of smoke from bodies
                as if no single

156

                                        self
                        could maintain
such a conflagration. But
                                the idea that cancels
                                        late arrival
                        at the developing sense
                        of insanity
could not be heard over
                        that choking silence.
Autumn leaves burned before they
                                                could fall.

Time to go inside after the
bell that marked the journey
                        by fire and four murdered
                                                flights,
                        a sequence
in consequence of the sky
                        looping around through
                                        Hades.
                                Building hulks
                        stand as memorial stones
over the bodies now incomplete
                                        stories
                        tolled earlier in terror.
                                People watch
                        TV's repeating pictures,
having only voices in their heads
to listen to, commonplace syllables.

                My bones, suddenly clay,
                        toppled over
                        a concrete step,
                        surprised, wondering how
                the airplane bombs could
reach me in Albuquerque
                        from New York.

157

Of course this was my own
                    poor vision.
In my office, I used pain
as an antidote for my own safety.
                    I didn't see my students:
                                        there was no class
                                                on 9/11.

That night I iced my thigh
                    during the critical intensity.
I harbored in myself a window
                    where blood seeped through
                                                the glass.
                    My swelling starting, pain
more intense, oddly welcome.
The World Trade Center never
                    sold its stock
                                that blistering day.
                                        It is now
                            its memory, monumental
where no unknown soldier
                                lies in clement ground.
                    Only firemen, police,
civilians beginning their business
                                                        day,
the phones dead, the voices speaking
through metaphysical dimensions,
                    unheard in the light.

That Civil War in Spain

Camel shadow on the wall.
Long moods that shift from orange

to black:
interest grows material and incandescent.
Motherwell's "Elegy
to the Spanish Republic" groans
as if still alive and in pain.
The way to take in huge death

by bombing
as a disease from
linkage to the feeling
of an idea but barely circumscribed
by the coefficient of rough black

shapes.

Somewhere a mood lapses
from the devil. Sources
congregate in small tumors
that betray blind apertures. Mind

focuses
on the time I was not
at Black Mountain ever, where
the writing lay
before me, joys
of trust in the grain.
Motherwell also froze power
into harsh granules, camel shadows
on the orange canvas

of a wall.

Goya's firing squad

aims
at Franco. The watch goes on
for a system to break logic into
fingers and elbows,

159

parts of the future edge
when spirit dominates
domination.
Still, the subject seeks carnal
embodiment. The wounded eye
looks beyond the dead
field of winter bones,
toward what can be found
in the sutures
that hold bodies
together.
Everywhere I hear a distant
throbbing as if the sublime
might lie in the breathing
body
next to mine.

No more than ever does the painting
suggest a means for approaching
the demonic mood.
Solitude must be exact, a bedrock against
the steep climb
into stringy air.
Spain was then
in Motherwell's compass
as he drove through
a nightmare: the insurgence against
life: Long live
death!
the one-armed, fascist general shouted
in the church where Unamuno
prayed.

How to bring light
from the subterranean echo that
dwindles with each
repetition.

160

The water
is hollow. No use
to prefer wisteria over snapdragons.
I have searched
the desert land for its roots
in the scorched earth. It is

surprising

that Motherwell's painting
fastens to that old civil war
and still believes that black
can enlighten the other

end

of the human telescope.

I never remember what

I said

after someone revealed a secret.
It is this nature I listen for
in art, as far as the sound

of battle

after it is done.
Silence, dried blood, the willful
destruction of history
that art digs out of the soil
with brush and lens.
Looking at Motherwell's

"Elegy,"

how to distinguish the camel
from the buffalo, animals that stand
and slowly move,

heavily move

across the orange

sun

as it goes down into the secret
graves of men
who fought for the same land,
listening to different prophets.

161

Gene Frumkin: Master of the Baffles

by John Tritica

"Each poetic word is thus an unexpected object, a Pandora's box from which fly out all the potentialities of language; it is therefore produced and consumed with a peculiar curiosity, a kind of sacred relish."
–*Roland Barthes,*
Writing Degree Zero

"Theoretic rush, thought filled with blood."
–*Nathaniel Mackey,*
"Song of the Andoumboulou 16"
Whatsaid Serif

"The story doesn't end here, where it ends."
–*Gene Frumkin,*"He is a Movie of Himself"

John Tritica

It is my good fortune to have had the friendship of an elder poet of singular vision, enormous talent, and vast erudition. As friend and mentor, his incisive critique of the art of poetry informed me in a way that enabled me to gain perspective on the shape of American poetry, including my own participation in it. Gene Frumkin was born on January 29, 1928 in New York, the Bronx, and moved to Los Angeles as a ten-year-old. After graduating from UCLA, Gene edited an apparel trade newspaper (from 1952-1966), during which time he began to write and publish poetry. In 1966, he moved to Albuquerque to teach at the University of New Mexico. What began as a one-year appointment to the English Department (replacing Robert Creeley), turned into a long and fruitful career of teaching and publishing, during which time he co-founded, with David Johnson, UNM's creative writing program, which included such notable writers as Joy Harjo, Leslie Marmon Silko, and Simon Ortiz. He retired in 1994, but taught occasional poetry workshops into the latter half of the 1990s. Gene's own work was included in varied publications, such as *Sulfur, Conjunctions, Poetry, Paris Review, boundary 2, Hambone, Caliban, Saturday Review, kayak, Poetry Northwest, The Best American Poetry 2002, Facture, Solo, Evergreen Review,* and *In Company: An Anthology of New Mexico Poets after 1960.* He published sixteen collections of poetry and a book is still forthcoming from Chax Press: *Meditations in Crowded Air.* (For further biographical details, I refer the reader to George Kalamaras' "Remembering Gene Frumkin," cited below.)

A number of us close to him last saw Gene at a party at my house the day before he died suddenly of a heart attack. Gene was less steady on his feet and couldn't drive at night for a good ten years, which is partially how I got to know Gene so well. We were part of a poetry circle called L)Edge, founded and driven by Mary Rising Higgins. We began meeting in 1986, and I was a founding member. Gene didn't join immediately; all of us were more like his students than his equals. I never studied formally with Gene at UNM, though he became a motivating source for me as poet, friend, and poetic guide. Gene was teaching in Hawaii for part of the late 1980s, so he didn't join until around 1989. By 1990 we shifted from meeting in a local (long since defunct) restaurant, to the friendlier homes of our members, all over the city of Albuquerque. Beginning in the mid-1990s I gave Gene rides, which would take up to twenty-five minutes in transit. Gene was a massively cultivated individual—his house on Mesa Verde was crammed with books, his bed surrounded by paperbacks, piled high. He went about the process of digesting leading edge ideas in a rather quiet way; his reading fed his teaching and poetry and thinking about the art. He enjoyed informing me of his poetics, which was one of his skills: analytical discussions about poetic strategies. While always advocating for the innovative, form-pushing side of poetry, Gene also read a great deal of "mainstream" poetry and fiction. In addition, he read widely in philosophy, aesthetic theory, literary theory, avant-garde fiction, biographies, crime and mystery novels, and a variety of poetry publications.

An introvert who loved to tell stories, Gene rose often to the occasion, and he was a great conversationalist, especially during

L)Edge sessions, in our car rides, or on the telephone. He not only critiqued work with a supportive fair-mindedness, but he also talked about the current state of poetry and what he was reading at the time, passing along recommendations. He was as good at listening as he was at talking, generously hearing out my ideas of poetry and what I was writing at the moment. Once I caught myself talking too much during a phone call, and I apologized for it. Gene agreed with me that I had talked too much, but then, after a twenty-second silence, added, "Don't let that stop you from expressing your insights out loud." That generosity illustrates his wise encouragement and stays with me as I continue to write.

As a beginner, Gene studied with the highly regarded poet Thomas McGrath, who recognized Gene's talent and proposed the not-very-revolutionary idea that a poem ought to surprise the reader. However, Gene's ability to integrate this principle fully into his practice is one of the supreme skills of his writing and one of the elements that makes his work supple and fresh—the practice of surprise. McGrath was known for a poetry of committed political radicalism, which, in its shorter lyrics, is sometimes metrically formal rhyming poetry, but in his masterwork *Letter to an Imaginary Friend,* he writes a long, at times rhapsodic, line of free verse. In fact, Gene uses rhyme a great deal in his first book, *The Hawk and the Lizard* (1963). From the late 1960s onward, Gene gives up rhyme, and his poetry has a different orientation from that of McGrath, who always encouraged his student. Gene's ear for tight clusters of sound and his exploration of the long line are informed by McGrath's practice. Although Gene would never formalize the principle of surprise in a theoretical essay, he writes a surprising, elusive, absurd, and powerful poetry from the late 1960s to his final works in 2007. In our conversations, he discussed how to employ language so that it can be read in multiple ways, a language that resists easy paraphrase, unfolding only over time. His approach to significance is that meaning is provisional, elusive, ambiguous, and shifting.

Indeed, Gene breaks up habitual perception that is rooted in rational thinking.

Some time in 1993 or so, Gene, in our conversations, introduced the term "baffles," or "the baffles," both verb and noun. Baffles are intended to upset the reader's routine or conventional expectations of what a poem ought "to do" or "mean." In the "Preface" to *Loops* (1979):

> *Loops* was composed on the basis of non-sequiturs, incongruities, and misconceptions....We are an over-interpretative society whose desire to 'understand' is matched only by its inability to do so, at least insofar as the rhythm of life and the depth of psyche are at issue....
> God is still present for some and for them serves as a repository of trust: where God rules there must be meaning. But meaning is a chameleon and even among the Godloving or Godfearing, as the case may be, there is no consensus (*Loops* n.p.).

Dry wit almost succeeds in concealing his strategy: sarcasm of tone acts to reinforce a sense of "radical openness" when it comes to significance in the poetry. A baffle is a strategic non-sequitur, and through his skilled use of the technique, the poet maintains tension and surprise in his work. Gene discussed his concept of the baffles during a few L)Edge meetings in the mid-90s, but mostly he used baffles as a form of defamiliarization that keeps the reader questioning. Gene frequently places some remote object or idea against an image that is immediately perceptible, and the greater the distance these objects or ideas stand from one another, the greater the power each has. There is a spirit of revolt in Gene's work, drawn from dada and surrealism. Gene's verse belongs in the thick of innovative contemporary poetry, because his work itself reveals a depth, rhythm, and wide-ranging significance, realized in its own language of tantalizing complexity.

Loops is composed of a series of surrealistic and satiric observations, where the narrator frequently speaks in the first person, building poetic "vignettes" that create their own havoc and delight, as we read:

> Repose on the banks
> of the Niagara River
>
>   on a blanket
>   on the grass
> I ate a small red sailboat
> That's all I remember
>   (6)

Throughout *Loops* there are no periods or commas, but where a verse sentence ends is indicated by the next sentence beginning with a capital letter. Within a collision of two "locations," memory is more an organ of creation, than one of recall. The absurdity is witty, grabs the reader's attention, and acts through a casual tone, as though the poet were providing a kind of ordinary recall of his diet on a given day.

Later in the book, he tells us:

> Philosophy ought to serve human needs
> like a waitress I discussed this with Linda
> a waitress at Sambo's She doesn't like
> her job Philosophy doesn't like its job either
> Two months later I learned they'd run off
> to Las Vegas together and become stars
>   (28)

A strange way of coupling people and livelihoods combines with a so-casual-it-is-absurd way of discussing philosophy and its work. Turning philosophy and a waitress into a cult of celebrities is very contemporary in tone. Such odd combinations are a hallmark of Gene's poetry.

I would like to go back in time to the title-poem of *The Rainbow-Walker* (1968), in order to demonstrate how Gene's poetry implements the baffles, prior to any articulation of the term. In the first four lines of the poem, he writes:

> My father the cold man in the darkness of the earth
> is a blue flame that keeps my hands alive
> I am heir to his station on the walrus-rock
> from which one sees the earth as if it ended many years
> ago (n.p.)

It is exactly this blue flame of surprise that keeps the poet's hands producing new poems. The invented compound, "walrus-rock," stretches out the significance. From a meditative position, the poet considers his inheritance in poetry. The speaker of the poem wishes to inherit his father's vision of the world. Later in the poem, the narrator declares his aim: "The theme is therefore Revolt[.]" But it's not the expected "Revolt" against the oppressive historical forces of our socio-economic structures that he rails, rather "Revolt against the corruptible franchise of the blood[.]" It's *ourselves*, our own limitations of thinking and feeling that we must break through. It's the power of our conventional thinking that we need to resist. It is a revolt against the corruptible and mechanistic view of the world, which posits prescriptive meanings and morals. Gene aims to break up rationalizations, because the tendency to follow routine blindly can rob life of its meaning. If the freshness and strangeness of the world can be presented in poetry, it is through revolt, a lynchpin of the baffles, keeping Gene's language in motion.

He concludes the poem by saying:

> Revolt the peaceful man's brother
> Rainbow across the waters of the dead
> But I walk so slowly my comradely image resembling my
> father
> Smiles up at me saying 'Walk faster walk on circusfoot
> Let your fist be olives and your eyes gazelles
> let your eyes be hammers
> When your toes touch the secret arc of the rainbow-circle
> All the colors are yours'

The ending of this poem rides on the word *circusfoot*, a neologism and baffle. The compound of these two familiar words kicks up several semantic notches, when they are combined as one in this poem. In the oracular voice of the poetic father, the eyes need to be both strong and swift so they might touch the full spectrum of colors. The *circusfoot* must be ever more fleet in the act of creation. As Gene's poetry stretches out, it becomes expansive, performing an alchemical transformation. In this way, the artist can bring to bear all the colors of invention to his palette.

When re-reading through the majority of Gene's work, I was drawn to the collection *The Old Man Who Swam Away and Left Only His Wet Feet* (1999), which brings together two long-out-of-print volumes of Gene's poetry, his fourth book, *Dostoevsky and Other Nature Poems* (1972), his ninth book *A Lover's Quarrel with America* (1985), and a selection of previously uncollected poems, *New Poems 1997*. In these poems Gene regards the page differently from his previous books. Most all of the first three books use justified left margins. In *Dostoevsky*, Gene approaches the page as an open field, where phrases form units, as perceptions follow one another in composition. This approach to the page represents an innovation in his work that he continues to develop over the next thirty-five years. Such composition is particularly compatible with Gene's use of baffles. As one example, I quote from the poem "Dostoevsky," which begins this way:

> When the river shines
> those nights of green translucent bones
> the bearded man fishes for stars   He groans in this labor
> which takes all his strength   What is hidden beneath the
> waters:
> a substance of moths
> (*Old Man* 27)

The third and fourth lines are justified left, but not the first, second, and fifth. The flexibility of this strategy gives Gene's body of work a kind of interweaving between uses of the margins.

Gene's rapidity of associations in the open field fit well with his skilled use of baffles. He employs two strategic baffles in these lines; in the first instance, the river's "green translucent bones" are placed right next to Dostoevsky who "fishes for stars"; in the second, the river's surface conceals "a substance of moths." We don't get directions in this poetry. Those who wish for a tidy paraphrase are destined to frustration here. Not Hemingway, but Dostoevsky is our fisherman. Still, nothing the narrator tells us identifies the Russian directly. By the final stanza, he writes:

> The bones of the river are his stars
> > they are ashes in his brain
> He is the icon the cauldron to whom we kneel in our
> > bones
> Beloved God beloved original of sin
> > who knows how to stab himself to the heart
> > > with his baited crosier
>
> (27)

Just when Gene appears to make some generalized philosophical statement in the first line of the quote, he pulls the rug out from underneath the reader's feet in the second: "they are ashes in his brain"—stars and ashes, diametrical opposites, maintain the poem's tension. Dostoevsky, who suffered epileptic seizures and dictated parts of his writing when seizures came on, also believed in the necessity of suffering as a vehicle for salvation. The poem likens Dostoevsky to a "cauldron" that affects the marrow of our bones. The final two lines are not biographical but deliver a striking impact of religious practices. A crosier is a highly stylized ceremonial staff, signifying high-ranking religious orders in the Catholic and Eastern Orthodox Church, in the latter of which Dostoevsky was a practicing believer. What keeps the poem in motion is the expression, "stab himself to the heart," not, *in* the heart, as is grammatically expected. An ambiguous image of power and suicide, the closure of the poem is no conclusion, but a conundrum which keeps the poem in motion.

In the next four books Gene writes in justified-left margins.[1] In *A Lover's Quarrel With America* (1985), he returns to using the open field composition in line and page. The titles alone, in a changed order, sound like one of Gene's poems: "Divagation From a Line in *The Aneid*," "In the Desert Alone at Night," "Androgyne in Aleph," "The Indian Capital of the World," "Arbitrary Design," "'Something,'" and "The Problem of Individual Identity is the Dilemma of Philosophy."

I don't think of Gene as a projectivist poet, but when Charles Olson and Robert Duncan use the page as body's geography, I am certain that Gene learned from his fellow poets, extending their approach to poetry in his own. He begins the poem "'Something'" like this:

> We want this to be about "something"
> a fact if possible
> or at least
>   a simulation
>   detachable
>
> like an organ   from the spherical music
>   from the supernal flesh
>
> It's how one says it
>
>   the system
>
>   where we live
>   our crowded intestines
>   reels of film entangled, cutting into one   another
>   no longer separable
>   as images
>   (*Old Man* 37)

Often readers expect the poem to be some direct unmediated representation of the world. Gene's poetry subverts this expectation, moving provisionally into and out of direct reference, reordering objects or ideas so suited to his use of baffles. The words are no detachable organs but recombinations of complex "reels" of thought and emotion impinging on one another. The emphasis on words themselves is orchestrated in a rhythm that renews what Gene began in *Dostoevsky and Other Nature Poems*. In encountering the field, our way of construing what happens in our lives is becoming more complex, crowding out our internal constructs, our films that reflect us. The skill here involves spacing in the composition of the poem, the rhythm of "It's how one says it," with heavy stress on *it*, which I take as the poetic act. Then "the system," as if floating in the middle of the poem, connects to the next stanza's "where we live. . ." This is how Gene brings something very remote to most people, "spherical music," and places it with something everyone feels at times: a stirring and churning in our entrails.

As usual Gene avoids officiating the tensions in his poem, which he concludes this way:

> Why then prolong this terminal discourse
> about "something"?

> It is enough to assent
> that heaven is androgynous
> and we are issues formed in time

> dyadic and processional
> Drapes around a nude figure
> in stone or air
> (37)

Gene evinces here a lack of patience with a "terminal discourse." Yet his contribution to the complex issue of how poetry is represented poses a conundrum, rather than an answer to the reader. As people evolve in time, do they act as concealment for the nude sculpture underneath? The closure of this poem is anything but conclusive. Another component of the practice of baffles is the poet's insistence on openness of closure, a technique Gene uses throughout his work.

171

In another poem in this collection, "Algorithm," Gene writes:

> The artificially intelligent human
> corresponds to a flow / a flaw in the sequence of
> whatever river
> is precisely like itself but never is
> (37)

This knot in our knowing is Gene's "target" throughout *A Lover's Quarrel with America*. For those who choose to expand their boundaries of knowing, Gene's work is replete with paradox, ambiguity, and recombinations of what we know with what we think we can know. Baffles act to keep the mind in motion. Are the "artificially intelligent" flow or flaw? What is the river that is never itself, exactly? Gene's poetry is structured around such paradoxes.

I haven't yet discussed Gene's *Clouds and Red Earth* (1981), which offers poems of place in imagery of closely observed New Mexico landscapes, enhanced by the poet's biographical particulars. Similarly in *New Poems 1997*, biographical details play an important role. Gene refers to a wide range of people in his life, from Uncle Hymie to Lydia ("my one wife"), from a high school teacher, to his son, Paul. There is a poignant tone to some of these poems (especially "Coming Home" and "The Family"), which reveal Gene's willingness to process personal struggles in poetic terms. Still the self-references are strategic, because they are often distanced through the prism of baffles, such as this nugget in "Ida," "I handle my thoughts arguably as marbles" (137). Or in "Correcting the Motion," "I look like myself / only when somebody quotes me" (142). Gene's open-field composition in *New Poems 1997* is what differentiates it from *Clouds and Red Earth* with its justified-left margins. It's not that the conventional margins rule out baffles, simply that Gene's elasticity of line in the open field finds an affinity for them.

Gene writes from what he calls "the speech appropriate / to silence" ("Saidless" 124). The poems take paradox as their

172

"subject." In "Uncle Hymie," for instance, Gene's uncle "cracked his head in Friedrichstadt / and became a natural surrealist". A brain-injury leads to being a surrealist? In "Under Depth," he writes, "I forget my name in the book of reason" (143). Gene's poetry acts as a celebration and defense of the great well of resources in the unconscious. His poetry plumbs the depths of the lived unconscious as a resource for poems.

"He is a Movie of Himself" is Gene's final poem, "fragmentary," yet over 300 lines, composed within no more than one month before dying, published posthumously in *Blue Mesa Review*, which he helped found. This final poem has a sublime absurdity, an inspired and constructed hilarity. "Movie" has a story, but no linear narrative. The speaker is incredibly familiar with Allen Ginsberg, his absurdist anti-hero. In "Movie," Gene recalls his first encounter with the fellow Jewish poet at a Ginsberg reading in the mid-1950s at the house of Mel Weisburd in Los Angeles; Gene handed Ginsberg's clothes back, after Ginsberg disrobed at the reading in response to a heckler. I quote the beginning long stanza:

> In thinking of Allen Ginsberg, I am ashamed to say
> that New York makes me cough. He is a maze whose exit
> startles
> the stairs to Heaven, and I fall amazed
> into his early poetry, rhyming like trees
> in an autumn woods. As I read on, his life
> displaces
> the morning star. I first heard of him
> in a bar where I was on my second drink. He stood
> naked
> before me
> on my third, his penis writing on the wall.
> Allen, I said, your poems wound me
> now that I read you, the sun going down.
> He never wrote to me. His name is rubber.
> ("Movie" 98)

Something modulates in his length and density of line: the units are longer, beautifully punctuated by the word "displaces" and the phrase "before me," lending the poem to story telling. In fact, moving away from the Bronx as a ten-year-old to grow up in Los Angeles, greatly improved Gene's asthma. The autobiographical details are presented to us freshly and humorously, in a conversational tone. Gene shows himself to be well read in Ginsberg's work, making references to the early rhyming poems, and then to "Howl," "Kaddish," and *The Fall of America*. Likewise, Gene uses Ginsberg's personal biography, such as his travels to India, his friendship with William Carlos Williams, and his contributions to Beat culture. Lest we try to give some shallow biographical reading to the poem, Gene begs us not to go down that road: "His name is rubber."

Later in the poem: "The long haste of Ginsberg's words prefigure Cendrars' 'Trans-Siberian . . . '" (103) Here Gene is playing with literary history; in 1913 the French modernist Blaise Cendrars published his lengthy narrative poem, which he called "The Prose of the Trans-Siberian and of Little Jeanne of France." Replete with phenomenal adventures in low-budget travelling, Cendrars' writings constitute a kind of proto-typical Beat ethos, prefiguring Ginsberg's international pilgrimages to the jungles of Bolivia, the ashrams of India, and the salons and cafés of Tangiers and Paris: "Blaise's one arm writes a big fire to endure / barely beyond the flame. / He is not a Beat drawing card, perhaps his French / goes off on a different journey" (103). The connection of Ginsberg and Cendrars is lightning quick, consonant with Pound's persuasion that all ages are contemporaneous. Cendrars' adventurousness, resourcefulness, and traveling lifestyle laid the pattern for Ginsberg, Neal Cassady, and Jack Kerouac. Gene also notes in "Movie," Louis Ginsberg, Allen's father, whose poetry submissions Gene and Mel (Weisburd) turned down as editors of *Coastlines*. It's not as though Gene became confessional, just more willing to discuss personal experience as a resource for poetic material, usually through the oblique lens of the baffles. It's this personal experience that creates much of the pathos of his later work. He draws us into his world, which includes the stories of his life, artistically altered. In order to provide a rich complexity, Gene also creates scenarios out of fabricated biography in "Movie," such as Ginsberg finding Van Gogh's ear in a Chinese restaurant. One of Gene's skills is as a non-linear storyteller, a teller of tales that only connect later.

At the conclusion of "He is a Movie of Himself," we see the parenthetic comment "(to be cont.)" Gene keeps his readers' inquiry moving through the use of baffles, a technique that stretches back at least as far as "The Rainbow-Walker" (1968). Though I considered *Loops* and "The Rainbow-Walker," two poems written in left-justified margins, it is the open field poems of *The Old Man Who Swam Away and Left Only His Wet Feet* (1998), and his final poem "He is a Movie of Himself" (2007) that provide the focus for my discussion of how Gene uses the page as a map, as it fans out, text rhythmically placed, separated by short units of phrasing, and then lengthened into non-linear story that is capable of registering a variety of tones from absurdity to poignancy.[2] Of course this places more interpretive weight on the reader. Gene's practice of interjecting the fantastic into the casual, and the remote with the everyday present is one quality that keeps his poetry alive, and kept him poetically lucid until he died. His poetry involves a strict avoidance of cliché and a willingness to use his own life stories filtered through baffles. Gene's poetic approach to language, story, biography and art constitutes a deeply cultivated accomplishment that adds to a discussion of innovative American poetry. As a friend, I grew to depend on his erudition and kindness and experience. As a reader of his poetry, my life as a poet is forever altered. Since we shared many of the same passions for individual poets, I was glad to have such reinforcement and inspiration from one of the great poets I'll ever have the privilege of knowing. I can't help thinking that since Gene passed so soon after we conversed with him, he pulled the final baffle on us, dying so suddenly, before we had an opportunity to say goodbye.

175

------

[1] *Locust Cry: Poems 1958-1965* (1973), *The Mystic Writing-Pad* (1977), *Loops* (1979), and *Clouds and Red Earth* (1981).
[2] In *Freud by Other Means* (2002), Gene also makes use of open field composition.

Works Cited

Barthes, Roland. *Writing Degree Zero*. Trans. Annette Lavers and Colin Smith. New York: Hill and Wang, 1967.

Cendrars, Blaise. *Complete Poems*. Trans. Ron Padgett. Berkeley, CA: Univ. California Press, 1992.

Frumkin, Gene. *The Hawk and the Lizard*. Denver: Alan Swallow, 1963.

---. *The Orange Tree*. Chicago: Cyfoeth, 1965.

---. *The Rainbow-Walker*. Albuquerque, NM: Grasshopper Press, 1968.

---.*Dostoevsky and Other Nature Poems*. San Luis Obispo, CA: Solo Press, 1972.

---. *Locust Cry: Poems 1958-1965*. Albuquerque, NM: San Marcos Press, 1973.

---. *The Mystic Writing-Pad*. Los Angeles: Red Hill Press, 1977.

---. *Loops*. Albuquerque, NM: San Marcos Press, 1979.

---. *Clouds and Red Earth*. Chicago: Swallow Press, 1981.

---. *A Lover's Quarrel with America*. Albuquerque, NM: Automatic Press, 1985.

---. *The Old Man Who Swam Away and Left Only His Wet Feet*. Albuquerque, NM: La Alameda Press, 1998.

---. *Freud by Other Means*. Albuquerque, NM: La Alameda Press, 2003.

---. "He is a Movie of Himself." *Blue Mesa Review* 20 (Fall 2007): 98-106.

Kalamaras, George. "*The Old Man who Swam Away and Left Only His Wet Feet*: Remembering Gene Frumkin." *Rain Taxi* 12, No. 2 (Summer 2007): 30-31.

Mackey, Nathaniel. *Whatsaid Serif*. San Francisco: City Lights Books, 1998.

McGrath, Thomas. *Letter to an Imaginary Friend*. Port Townsend, WA: Copper Canyon Press, 1997.

Gary L. Brower
Escalating Through The Labyrinth*
(For Gene Frumkin, 1928-2007)

*"Time limps behind the escalator, Freud
with a stopwatch, Jung with a camera."*
— Gene Frumkin, "Escalator."

*"I too am a myth...Walking the labyrinth is
an ancient spiritual exercise."*
— G.F., "Narrative of Conscience."

*"I want to fuck you, I want to fuck all
the parts and places, I want you all of me."*
— Lenore Kandel, "Love Lust Poem."

I

Soixante Neuf was a good year for Lenore
          her verse and controverse exploding like
     a hidden aneuryism of the Self
                    outraging hypocrites
who claim God-children are created by a Star in the East
     when it causes Immaculate Combustion
          denying society is an organasm
     of linear and circular joining
          for multiplication of nuclei.

This wasn't the saintly Lenore from the Poe House
          named by angels
     of whom Edgar and the Ravens doo-wopped:
"Lenore, Lenore, Nevermore, Nevermore
     Lenore, Lenore, Nevermore, Nevermore"
but a new Persona
     who wanted sex with the lights on
          all over the globe.

177

The escalator waits for no one
             and Lenore was riding it
         carrying her two lapdogs
              Sigmund and Karl
                     one under each arm
Karl yapping on the way up
           Sigmund on the way down
      both punished when necessary
         by a whack with the Golden Bough.

II

In the shadow of the Hotel Libido
              Feodor's twisted smile is cast like a
net over sleepwalkers
who order in from the Ego's dining room
         while the children of Prince Mishkin
and Princess Psyche   the animated little ziggies
      including the Cutest of the Cute   the charming
Mandala
        are singing *La Cucaracha* on *karaoke* night
     in the Lobe Room of the hotel bar
       using the professional name : Psychic Rugrats.
Afterward   eight and a half of them   if we include the
dwarf
         circle-danced on a beach dressed as clowns
          under the watchful Third Eye of the White
Sheik
        as film director Federico Fellatio was known.
    Then they chased Lenore down a maze of halls in the
spa-palace at Marienbad
        where mirrors reflect mirrors
           in a non-stop Moebius filmstrip
   up and down escalators through the labyrinth
         getting it up on one   down on the
other.

Sigmund and Karl sniff around in the shadows like
bloodhounds of the dream
        their labyrinth illuminated by Sirius
     whose light is more that its bark
       in its incarnation as the Dog Star
    Canis Major   the God-Dog of the galaxy both inside
and out.

If Kafka's world was a nightmare
          who owns Lenore's worldwide wet
dream?
        How many imagine they dream of having a
nightmare
     in which Lenore steps on Gregor Samsa
            like a cockroach in daylight?
     As it says in the *Talmud* a dream not understood
           is like a letter unopened
or in psychiatric terms a crotch unzipped
     where you need to know when a cigar is just a Vienna
sausage.

III

In the Oedipal *bazouki* between *anima* and *animus*
     in the See and Noh of masks
         the painted *Kabuki* faces catalogued by
Sigmund and Karl
        Government Archetypes want to see your *Id*
         that is   your ID
    because your dreams are your identity
     and they want to twist them
        so you come into their control.
    Lenore's poem   they say   won't pass through
Customs
     at the border of hypocrisy and camoflage.

IV

In the poet's corner   with Golden Gloves on
            ready for the joust
    you pull out the weapon of your imagination
                like Ossip Mandelstam
    confronting the deified patriarch of the Stalinist Orthodox
Church.
But here it's the First Church of the Hypocrite whose adherents
        kill your soul in order to save it
                while trying to burn words in your mouth
                    like books they throw on bonfires.

            As the epic Green Knight defending the Exiled
Lyric Lenore
                you were Sir Gawain disguised as Don
Quixote
        confronting the Windmill with your Trojan shield and
phallic lance
                and she became your Dulcinea-babe who
says:
                "Sometimes a Hole is more than the sum of the
other parts"

            But if your dream turns nightmare
                say   you are on an escalator and the
steps suddenly
            go flat halfway up
                        or down and the moving handrail
                turns into a sharp knife
        you may awaken to hear the voice of Sigmund
    saying: "Sometimes an escalator is just an escalator"
                as he monitors the heartbeat of your footsteps
                while Karl takes your photo
            at the end of the escalator marathon.

180

When the Superego tried to suppress Lenore's lusty lyrics
you read them out for everyone to hear
releasing them like balloons into the collective
unconcious.

As Walcott said
"poetry is always treason if it tells the truth"
and if it doesn't it's not poetry.
In the Van Gogh ear of historical

memory

which I pick up like a conch shell on a beach
I hear the Andrews Sisters singing
Bei mir bist du schoen
Bei mir bist du schoen
Bei mir bist du schoen.

---

*This poem refers to the 1969 controversy at the University of New Mexico over Lenore Kandel's "Love Lust Poem." Right-wing politicians and religious leaders were offended by the inclusion of the poem in a literature class, wanted to ban it and punish the university. The poem was then banned from campus by the Regents. This led to the faculty in all classes writing the poem on classroom blackboards and reading it to classes. Gene Frumkin opposed the attempt to suppress the poem and at one point read it aloud on campus at a large protest gathering. The English Department chairman was removed, the University budget was reduced and those funds were used for an investigation by the state legislature.

The quote at the end of the poem is from Nobel poet Derek Walcott. The two epigraphs from Gene's poems are from his book *Freud by Other Means*. This poem was first read at a tribute reading for Gene held at the Anasazi Fields Winery in Placitas, NM, in April, 2007.

George Kalamaras

I'm Writing Gene a Letter

In memory of Gene Frumkin

I'm writing Gene a letter but he's dead.
I keep trying to say it's 99
in Fort Collins today but only 93
in Albuquerque. I keep trying his side
with my hand, the resurrection of his word.
Remember the Indian who sold us cedar?
I had a headache three days and could kill it
only in Livermore after dumping
the bundle from my backseat.

Remember the fragrance of the full moon
over Dodge? I'm writing Bob my mouth,
the tender of it and clutch. The way this word
or that. The moist imprint of my strain.
Trains don't always reach West, I'd say,
and he'd nod that rain-in-the-barrel nod
he'd use as table water in Vermont, Susan
each evening at the stitch, dirty shirt
left out on the truck to wash and dry.

I can't write Álvaro because I love him.
No one can write another they see
as themselves. No one agrees. Nothing.
Not even the pronouns. So I'm writing
Álvaro through Gene because Bob
just published his book. Álvaro's book,
not Gene's. Made by Bob's hand.
My book in a way. And Tom McGrath's,
because he kept writing Gene
a note. I keep writing

John because he's not dead, because he writes me
back each day as if I'm answering myself,
as if he's unleashed the fire ants
of Namibia again in my wrist.
In a way I'm writing Bob, though sometimes I call
him Patrick. I begin, *Dear Rain-in-My-Chest,*
or *Dear Zhivago platting the full Yuriatan moon
over Dodge,* or *Sad, Sad Glance of the Owl.*
I call Patrick a name. My name. Paul's.
Barney. Bootsie. Adorable-Beagle-Breath.
Because Gene loved them both,
though he died before Bootsie arrived.

I can't write Gene because he's alive.
Somewhere busy. Marking my strain.
He keeps saying, *Hey, amigo, don't write me
anymore. I'm fried. Write Bob,* though they never met.
I think Gene wants to write Álvaro
so is asking me to write Bob.
I think John wants to live in DeKalb
forever, even if it's not the West,
maybe because I'm writing him
how much I need to stay alive.
I think how Patrick and Paul loved Barney
and will love her even more
through Bootsie when they meet.
Bob loves them all in his rain-in-the-barrel
way, and through Kokomo, his cat,
who keeps napping as if Gene hasn't died.
As if Bob has left Vermont
and is capturing the full moon
over Dodge from a train that keeps trying
the loping rails West.

So I'll visit Álvaro in New Mexico
and not write. A letter, that is,

though I'll still skill the sky.
Because I love him, as I love Gene,
even though Gene's tired of me
disturbing his rest. Though it's eternal,
so one more letter can't mean much.
Maybe I'll write Eric
before seeing Álvaro because Gene loved Eric
too. Even before Gene died.
As he loved my wrist. The one red
with ants swollen in bitten blood.
The blood John sends back to me each day
when he writes to help me somehow stay alive.

assemblage sculpture by William Georgenes

Carlos

Carlos is his name, and he walks as if he has not slept for days.

"Bro'" he says excitedly, "this is sick. 99% of the people do not
      care,
but the 1% inside baseball
people are jacked. Here is the deal bro': I will hit it hard over the
next 2 months, build my practice
up, then go to DC, meet with the big boys, then do some polling
      to see
where I stand—"

His car with a busted tail light, door low to the pavement like
      how he
roams the House Floor, or
alert and ready for the Speaker to call on him, standing there
      with the
microphone. His dizzying
worlds crash into his cell phone, making me tired.

It is a preacher's cadence, what he does: "I respectfully...." A
prolonged pause, as on the panel
we await his vote. "Move to table." Or when he said: "But the
      haters,"
the pause again. "Will do
what they do."

Shrinking the mundane into a workable formula, I mimic out of
      tribute.
He presents a truly
original figure, always quick to joke, his dark circles upstaged by
      his
ready smile, lean and
pensive in his tennis shoes and suit, all street.

"I should have pulled the trigger long ago. But I am just a
      bachelor,

bro'....living off the land."

People like us grade each other on the crescent moon. People like
        us
dream in a philanthropic
way, believing the lessons as we did.

Scholarships await at the Bull Ring. Medium rare.

Bill O'Neill
Revisiting Ithaca In A Dream

Something deep within resisted having a life that could be
        neatly filed
into the Olin Stacks.

Now I wear my favorite denim shirt, shredded, and worn laced-
        up boots
that my college pal
does not understand, as I never understood our jock language
        which might
as well have been
Navajo.

Fierce in my privacy, we talk about the missed reunions and
        high school
admissions and the
sheer volume of what was just never my deal.

My answer: show me, at the very least, a full and defiant moon
        that does
not dissolve into the
resignation of the next morning.

My college friend sniffs my backpack, makes a face, then smiles
        through
his sunglasses:

"Wall Street for me. Greyhound for you. Isn't life beautiful?"

Like a burning eucalptyus tree, with its thick black smoke.

Idea Vilariño
I'm Calling You

Love
from shadow
from pain
love
I'm calling you
from the asphyxiating well of memory
with nothing that helps me nor waits for you.
I'm calling you
love
like calling destiny
or a dream
of peace
I'm calling you
with my voice
with my body
with my life
with everything I have
with desperation
with thirst
with weeping
as if you were air
and I were drowning
as if you were light
and I were dying.
From a dark night
from oblivion
from hours closed
on loneliness
without tears or love
I'm calling out to you
as if to death
love
as if to death.

---

translation by Gary L. Brower

Idea Vilariño
Not Now

Now it won't be
not now
we won't live together
I won't raise your child
nor sew your clothes
I won't have you at night
nor kiss you when leaving
you'll never know who I was
why others loved me.
I'll never know
why nor how never
nor if it were true
what you said it was
nor who you were
nor who I was for you
nor how it might have been
living together
loving each other
waiting for us
to be.
Now I'm no more than myself
forever and you
now
won't be for me
more than you. You are not
in a future day
I will not know where you live
with whom
nor if you remember.
You will not embrace me ever
like tonight
never.
I will never touch you again.
I will not see you die.

––––––

translation by Gary L. Brower

Jonathan Slator
Above the Mist

Great days may dawn ill.

A while to strike a fire in the drizzle,
kindling wet, matches failing to flare,
the bull elk guffawing from the close pines
through the fog.

From camp, climbing in dense mist
over damp bracken, a clutch of grosbeaks
chattering in the birches, wondering if the day will be lost

in this shroud. Struggling upward, the rasp of the lungs
heralding the approach of the seventh decade,
racing the cloud up the ridge, till the heart
worries the ribs.
I concede
sprawling to watch the curtain rise.

And there
prosceniumed by the stratum is the mountain bowl
and beyond, the volcanoed plain,
strafed by Blakesian shafts.
From below the crag a grey arrow rifles north.
I look down on the slate back of a falcon

hunting birds. She loops the cirque thrice
then stoops talons fisted to sever the grosbeak
in a pink shock of down. Spurred by the show
I clamber up through strewn drapes
the valley now clear, now gone.
The stag braying, now and then.

Above the last mutilated pine
at the raw saddle
ravens kite the gale,
bickering like fish wives.

I johnmuir the ridge, shepherding a flock of big horns.
The ewes and lambs dash the arête
strafed by a pair of harpies
striving to pitch a sheep or two
into the abyss but the beasts survive.
The eagles bank away and know the distant ridge
in the time it takes me to trudge

a few steps. The light rakes the range.
I quit the tops
with regret and stumble down a tilted wood
lured by the bugle. Stalking amongst the trunks
I spot the cows browsing
then the tines of the bull, six and seven. His head tosses
in disquiet, aware of an alien aroma, he herds

his harem away. Thrilled I rest on an outcrop
glimpsing the gang in the brush.
Then the crash of a broken branch
the cows stampede under the rock.
The bull goading them
charges so close beneath me

that if I were a caballero or young or Artemis
I could drop on his back
cling to his antlers
and steer him joyfully through the forest.

But I am none of those.
At camp I squat by the fire
the tea ambrosial
the light lambent,
the mood lacking language to match.

Jonathan Slator

The Ghost of Cochise

Coming down from the climb
in failing light
ropes bandoliered,
like bandits heading for a train,
we pass the apache pantheon

its huge rock arrowhead teetering
in uncertain balance.
a flicker of shadow fools the eye.
The ghost of Cochise

returned to grieve the death
of half his family
at the hand of the fool, Lieutenant Bascom?
Then emerging, face daubed
to wreak one last gory

saturnalia on gringo and mexicano alike
and to ring the knell
on a way of life
where a man won standing through

the depth of his generosity
the savagery of his close combat
the permanence of his bond
but lost it through
duplicity, cowardice, greed,
niceties marking many of the civilized
men of the time.

Hannah Craig
Minnows

From the brooked barbed-wire of the fence
I watch the little fish
redirect themselves around each barrier
as one,
as if they learned from the very nature
of water. As if these were light bulbs,
drawn in layers, not gobstoppers in pipe drains,
in hedges of cattail and foxtail,
nor angular, dark-headed logs,
jaws prehensile, focused from nowhere.
These,
like laughter, malleable, quick.
Nothing is required to direct them or to stem them;
they fledge
at the boundaries of sunlight, lolling
in gold pulled from that early moment of creation,
bristling at once in every new direction,
feathered by the breezy current.
In their wake, in mine, in wakefulness itself,
having seen them, I am pulled. Pressures
from sandstone aquifers, from claps
of the hand, from the cow's nose, buried to the root,
the slaloming cords of brightness about her head.
I am not free for I am pulled.
My tread is heavy; o pity me, my feet have nearly been
my soul.

Wayne Lee
Truck Stop Theory

To prove your premise that trucker cafes
do not in fact offer the very finest
in late-night cuisine along the interstate,
you pull our compact rental rig up
at Travelers Oasis, its gaudy neon display
promising "America's Best Truck Stop."

We peruse souvenir jackalope coffee mugs,
imitation turquoise-inlaid pocketknives
and Hell's Canyon shot glasses, then slide
into a frayed vinyl booth, its tar-stained
ashtrays half-filled with Marlboro butts,
its table tent touting Bud Lite. Our waitress
for the evening is Jackie, who actually pops
her gum and calls us "hon." You order
chicken-fried steak and fries, I risk
the Fettucine Alfredo chef's special,
get a pile of congealed noodles
bigger than my head. We forego dessert.

"See?" you gloat, then saunter off to buy
your wife a miniature personalized Idaho
license plate while I, in mute acceptance
of the irrefutable truth, step outside
for a breath of diesel smoke before taking
the wheel and heading on down the pike
for Mountain Home.

Jill A. Oglesby
At the Funeral of My Father
November 2005

At the funeral of my father, the fighting has stopped.
My mother, brother, and I in the front row
are three sparrows that flew into window glass.

Dad's nose is wrong. The undertaker pinched it in.
"O mhíorbhuil gráis, nach briagha an céol...."*
At the moment I sing, some people are surprised

to know Tom had a daughter.
The American flag-draped coffin, the best gray suit.
Dad's picture from the army–a fresh-faced carnation.

The piper plays "Amazing Grace" and walks away on the 2nd
          verse,
and I watch my father walk into his younger self
in Waxahachie, Texas, in the town square barbershop,

1950's Chevies, and my mother walks by in her Mandarin dress.
He turns and raises his hand goodbye to me, grinning.
In the receiving line, these are blossoms in the hand: kind words

from the Quilters, the Cloggers, the 12-steppers, the
          Elderhostelers,
and at the house later, we're laughing about playing
"Take Me Out to the Ballgame" at the funeral.

Should've quoted the Boy Scout oath. This is what it means
to be Human: to go back to the house for a meal,
to have bitter arguments and high ideals not shared by loved
          ones.

This is what it means to be Human—so many things
outside our control, our incomplete understanding.
Seven days from diagnosis of "terminal" to death.

I haven't been inside this house for 8 years.
Everyone likes my sweet potato tarts.
They tell me I'm beautiful. I am this man's daughter.

---

*Scots Gaelic for "Amazing Grace, how sweet the sound."

196

Jill A. Oglesby
Visiting

My father sits down for a chat.
He still has that pinched-in nose from the undertaker
which makes his voice sound a little nasal

but deep. "When we let go of physical existence...."
he says, and in his eyes shines out
a knowledge beyond all I've ever seen.

So, I sit with him awhile
and accept him as he is, even though
he made nuclear weapons, which is all over now.

We remember together when he bought me a power saw,
a well-weighted hammer, a pipe wrench,
screwdrivers, a ratchet wrench, and vise grips.

We laugh. I never bought that house in Florida,
but I love my tools. On his visit,
we sat in his rental car talking

as the moon rose over Lake Alachua.
Live oaks were grand old women shawled in Spanish moss
and alligators moved as tiles in a children's plastic car game.

"Dad," I say, "you weren't the easiest father to have."
But, he knows that.
He really does know everything now.

Librotraficante *poetry reading at Albuquerque's*
National Hispanic Cultural Center, March 15, 2012

Smuggling Books
Behind The Saguaro Curtain

On March 4 and March 15, two poetry readings were held in
Albuquerque to raise funds, to raise consciousness, and to protest
the campaign instigated in the Tucson School District by Arizona
officials to ban books used in the Mexican-American Studies high
school curriculum. And to protest the abolition of that whole pro-
gram, which had been very successful in galvanizing its students
not only to succeed in school but to go on to higher learning.

Was it that success that led to the attack by Right-Wing Repub-
licans who control the Arizona government at this time? Or is
it the usual divide-and-conquer tactic used everywhere by the
so-called "conservatives" to create "wedge issues" between parts
of the general populace to gain power? Or is it simply racism?
Or a combination of all three? Whatever it is, it fits into a pat-
tern of attempts to repress the Hispanic population of the state
(now estimated at 30%), to keep control in Anglo hands. It is, in

other words, a majoritarian oppression of Arizona's largest non-Anglo minority whose growth is seen as a threat. It is part of a nationwide campaign to attack education, schools, teachers, their unions and textbooks, in order to weaken education in general and to rewrite history for Right-Wing propaganda purposes. For example, in Tennessee they are trying to eliminate any reference to slavery in that state's history textbooks, and in Texas to expunge the textbook chapter on the national Civil Rights movement and the leadership of Dr. Martin Luther King, Jr. Arizona has a long history of persecution of Native Americans, and later, of African-Americans. So they have experience in repressing minorities. They can't get rid of Native American Studies because of a Federal mandate related to that past discrimination. But at least two major Native American writers in the state have been very active in the opposition to these recent attacks on ethnic studies: Simon Ortiz and Leslie Marmon Silko.

Divisive politicians, appealing to prejudices and ignorance, link the Hispanic people of the state to the issue of "illegal immigration." And then they connect that issue with drug smugglers crossing the Mexico-Arizona border, trying to equate them with economic migrants. It is a way to target Hispanics with false associations, whether they are citizens or not. This is guilt by association couched in racist terms and applied to non-Anglos by the people whose ancestors stole the land from Native Americans and Hispanics in the first place. Regarding the latter, there was the trumped-up US-Mexican War of 1846-48. This war, an attempt by southern slave-holder President James K. Polk to annex territory so as to expand slavery as well as the national territory, was denounced by Abraham Lincoln, John Quincy Adams, Henry David Thoreau, and the Whig Party for what it was. The war was justified on grounds of "Manifest Destiny," that is, that Anglo Americans were blessed by God as a Chosen People, and had the right to steal territory from other nations or do whatever they want. It was the beginning of official justifications of "American Exceptionalism" which is today "Anglo Exceptionalism" in Arizona (and certain other locations). Interestingly, Arizona was settled in part by a large number of southerners (before but especially after the Civil War), who brought their tradition of racism with them. During the Civil War, southern sympathesizers called a convention, which met in Tucson, and declared Arizona to be a Confederate Territory.

Today, these efforts to control minority groups are being driven by several Arizona Republican politicians, including Governor Jan Brewer, Attorney General Tom Horne and State Superintendant of Education John Huppenthal. They have been manuevering for a couple of years to do exactly what they did this year in Tucson. The fact that they have zeroed in on Mexican-American Studies is related to that growing segment of the population that could threaten their political power. Ultimately, Huppenthal and Horne threatened the Tucson District with the loss of state funds if they didn't comply with new laws passed especially to eliminate ethnic studies programs and other cultural underpinnings of the Hispanic community. This fits in with the racist policies of Maricopa County Sheriff Joe Arpaio, SB 1070, and other racist laws passed by the legislature.

When it came to the book banning, the Tucson Unified School District (TUSD) School Board seems to have been willingly complicit with the politicians. School administrators entered the classrooms and took the books from the hands and desks of the students and locked them up in school libraries. The students, 60% of whom are Hispanic in the District, walked out of the schools day after day in protest, the teacher's union has sued, and protests have arisen all over the U.S. and even abroad. The TUSD has said that they didn't ban books but simply locked up books used in classes deemed by Huppenthal to be "out of compliance" with those new state laws. In addition, teachers were told that all books on the subjects discussed in the cancelled classes were not to be presented to the students by teachers at any time, in any classes. TUSD administrators stated there was no banning of books, just the banning of a program in which the books were used. Students could, they said, check any of the books out from the library, but this was more than discouraged, according to teachers.

The reason for ethnic studies classes in Arizona is clear: the culture and history of minority ethnic groups in the state are not discussed in the regular textbooks. Huppenthal and his allies set up laws that say that anything other than Anglo history is not valid, is un-American, encourages race hatred and the overthrow of the U.S. Government. We are back to the 1950s when McCarthyism perpetrated the same paranoid mentality. And to cap off the controversy, Sean Arce, an award-winning teacher who headed the TUSD Mexican-American Studies program was recently fired. These same politicians now say they may turn to similar programs in the state's universities. University of Arizona professor Roberto Rodriguez has said that this entire campaign against the Hispanic population of the state by Horne, Huppenthal and their ilk is a "civilizational war" in which Horne has said that Mexican culture is not Greco-Roman based and therefore not within Western civilization. Rodriguez compares the Tucson events with the Spanish destroying Mayan codices in the Yucatan of 1562. It is an attempt to destroy native culture in order to perpetuate Anglo hegemony.

All of the books used in any classes of the Mexican-American Studies programs were outlawed by TUSD, and they focused on seven titles for particular attacks. To fight back against this repression, Hispanic writers and leaders in various states organized protests. The most extensive effort is the *Librotraficante* (book smugglers) Caravan. This caravan left Houston, TX, led by Liana López and Tony Díaz (of the *Nuestra Palabra* latino writer's organization) on March 12, heading west for Tucson, to bring the banned books (called "wetbooks") back to the students there and establish "clandestine libraries." A local coordinating committee in Albuquerque organized in tandem with the Houston caravan. On March 4, a poetry reading at The Outpost jazz club raised the issues before the Houston *Librotraficante* caravan arrived for a larger event on March 15. Local poets reading at the March 4 event included Levi Romero (New Mexico's Centennial Poet), Margaret Randall, Andrea Serrano, Carlos Contreras, Yasmin Najimi, Mary Oishi, Tanaya Winder, Richard Vargas, Brian Hendrickson, Jessica Helen López, Don McIver, Hakim Bellamy, and Gary L. Brower. More than 150 attended. The event was sponsored by John Crawford's West End Press.

Before arriving in Albuquerque on March 15, the Caravan stopped in San Antonio for a rally, then for a press conference in El Paso, and another press conference in Mesilla/Las Cruces (with New Mexico's well-known writer Denise Chavez), and finally at the house of Rodolfo Anaya, who gave them copies of his books to distribute to students in Tucson. From Anaya's Albuquerque residence, the Caravan activists proceeded to the National Hispanic Cultural Center, where the protest poetry reading was taking place with an estimated 400 in attendance. The local poets who read at the NHCC included: E. A. "Tony" Mares, Cathy Arellano, Levi Romero, Mary Oishi, Gary L. Brower, Hakim Bellamy, Richard Vargas (who served as MC for these events), Margaret Randall, Andrea Serrano, and Bill Nevins. After the arrival of the Houston Caravan bus, members of that traveling group came up to the stage and also read poems, headed up by Tony Díaz. More than three thousand dollars was raised between the two events to help with the distribution of the banned books in Tucson. The audience was very appreciative of the poets and united in support of the Caravan to Tucson, preparing them to start out the next day, to smuggle their banned books into Tucson, past the Saguaro Curtain.   —GLB

LIST OF BANNED BOOKS IN TUCSON UNIFIED SCHOOL DISTRICT
Source: http://drcintli.blogspot.com/2012/01/tusd-banned-books-lists.html

High School Course Texts and Reading Lists Table 20: American Government/Social Justice Education Project 1, 2 - Texts and Reading Lists
- Rethinking Columbus: The Next 500 Years (1998) by B. Bigelow and B. Peterson
- The Latino Condition: A Critical Reader (1998) by R. Delgado and J. Stefancic
- Critical Race Theory: An Introduction (2001) by R. Delgado and J. Stefancic
- Pedagogy of the Oppressed (2000) by P. Freire
- United States Government: Democracy in Action (2007) by R. C. Remy
- Dictionary of Latino Civil Rights History (2006) by F. A. Rosales
- Declarations of Independence: Cross-Examining American Ideology (1990) by H. Zinn

Table 21: American History/Mexican American Perspectives, 1, 2 - Texts and Reading Lists
- Occupied America: A History of Chicanos (2004) by R. Acuña
- The Anaya Reader (1995) by R. Anaya
- The American Vision (2008) by J. Appleby et el
- Rethinking Columbus: The Next 500 Years (1998) by B. Bigelow and B. Peterson
- Drink Cultura: Chicanismo (1992) by J. A. Burciaga
- Message to Aztlán: Selected Writings (1997) by R. Gonzales
- De Colores Means All of Us: Latina Views Multi-Colored Century (1998) by E. S. Martínez
- 500 Años Del Pueblo Chicano/500 Years of Chicano History in Pictures (1990) by E. S. Martínez
- Codex Tamuanchan: On Becoming Human (1998) by R. Rodríguez
- The X in La Raza II (1996) by R. Rodríguez
- Dictionary of Latino Civil Rights History (2006) by F. A. Rosales
- A People's History of the United States: 1492 to Present (2003) by H. Zinn

Course: English/Latino Literature 7, 8
- Ten Little Indians (2004) by S. Alexie
- The Fire Next Time (1990) by J. Baldwin
- Loverboys (2008) by A. Castillo
- Women Hollering Creek (1992) by S. Cisneros
- Mexican White Boy (2008) by M. de la Peña
- Drown (1997) by J. Díaz
- Woodcuts of Women (2000) by D. Gilb
- At the Afro-Asian Conference in Algeria (1965) by E. Guevara
- Color Lines: "Does Anti-War Have to Be Anti-Racist Too?" (2003) by E. Martínez
- Culture Clash: Life, Death and Revolutionary Comedy (1998) by R. Montoya et al
- Let Their Spirits Dance (2003) by S. Pope Duarte
- Two Badges: The Lives of Mona Ruiz (1997) by M. Ruiz
- The Tempest (1994) by W. Shakespeare
- A Different Mirror: A History of Multicultural America (1993) by R. Takaki
- The Devil's Highway (2004) by L. A. Urrea
- Puro Teatro: A Latino Anthology (1999) by A. Sandoval-Sánchez & N. Saporta Sternbach
- Twelve Impossible Things before Breakfast : Stories (1997) by J. Yolen
- Voices of a People's History of the United States (2004) by H. Zinn

Course: English/Latino Literature 5, 6
- Live from Death Row (1996) by J. Abu-Jamal
- The Lone Ranger and Tonto Fist Fight in Heaven (1994) by S. Alexie
- Zorro (2005) by I. Allende
- Borderlands La Frontera: The New Mestiza (1999) by G. Anzaldua

- A Place to Stand (2002), by J. S. Baca
- C-Train and Thirteen Mexicans (2002), by J. S. Baca
- Healing Earthquakes: Poems (2001) by J. S. Baca
- Immigrants in Our Own Land and Selected Early Poems (1990) by J. S. Baca
- Black Mesa Poems (1989) by J. S. Baca
- Martin & Mediations on the South Valley (1987) by J. S. Baca
- The Manufactured Crisis: Myths, Fraud, and the Attack on America's Public Schools (1995) by D. C. Berliner and B. J. Biddle
- Drink Cultura: Chicanismo (1992) by J. A. Burciaga
- Red Hot Salsa: Bilingual Poems on Being Young and Latino in the United States (2005) by L. Carlson & O. Hijuielos
- Cool Salsa: Bilingual Poems on Growing up Latino in the United States (1995) by L. Carlson & O. Hijuelos
- So Far From God (1993) by A. Castillo
- Address to the Commonwealth Club of California (1985) by C. E. Chavez
- Women Hollering Creek (1992) by S. Cisneros
- House on Mango Street (1991) by S. Cisneros
- Drown (1997) by J. Díaz
- Suffer Smoke (2001) by E. Díaz Bjorkquist
- Zapata's Discipline: Essays (1998) by M. Espada
- Like Water for Chocolate (1995) by L. Esquievel
- When Living was a Labor Camp (2000) by D. García
- La Llorona: Our Lady of Deformities (2000), by R. García
- Cantos Al Sexto Sol: An Anthology of Aztlanahuac Writing (2003) by C. García-Camarilo et al
- The Magic of Blood (1994) by D. Gilb
- Message to Aztlan: Selected Writings (2001) by Rodolfo "Corky" Gonzales
- Saving Our Schools: The Case for Public Education, Saying No to "No Child Left Behind" (2004) by Goodman et al
- Feminism is for Everybody (2000) by b hooks
- The Circuit: Stories from the Life of a Migrant Child (1999) by F. Jiménez
- Savage Inequalities: Children in America's Schools (1991) by J. Kozol
- Zigzagger (2003) by M. Muñoz
- Infinite Divisions: An Anthology of Chicana Literature (1993) by T. D. Rebolledo & E. S. Rivero
- ... y no se lo trago la tierra/And the Earth Did Not Devour Him (1995) by T. Rivera
- Always Running - La Vida Loca: Gang Days in L.A. (2005) by L. Rodríguez
- Justice: A Question of Race (1997) by R. Rodríguez
- The X in La Raza II (1996) by R. Rodríguez
- Crisis in American Institutions (2006) by S. H. Skolnick & E. Currie
- Los Tucsonenses: The Mexican Community in Tucson, 1854-1941 (1986) by T. Sheridan
- Curandera (1993) by Carmen Tafolla
- Mexican American Literature (1990) by C. M. Tatum
- New Chicana/Chicano Writing (1993) by C. M. Tatum
- Civil Disobedience (1993) by H. D. Thoreau
- By the Lake of Sleeping Children (1996) by L. A. Urrea
- Nobody's Son: Notes from an American Life (2002) by L. A. Urrea
- Zoot Suit and Other Plays (1992) by L. Valdéz
- Ocean Power: Poems from the Desert (1995) by O. Zepeda

UPDATE, Monday, January 16, 2012
- Bless Me Ultima by Rudolfo Anaya
- Yo Soy Joaquin/I Am Joaquin by Rodolfo Gonzales
- Into the Beautiful North by Luis Alberto Urrea
- The Devil's Highway by Luis Alberto Urrea

E. A. "Tony" Mares
Ode to *los librotraficantes*

You carry books as you roll along
in your caravan through Texas, New Mexico,
and on to Arizona. You are
the most dangerous caravan in America.

Once your ancestors crossed the Río Grande,
their bodies wet from the swirling water,
the sweat running down their backs.
Now you carry wet books in your caravan,
books dripping with wisdom. You are

the most dangerous caravan in America.
You scatter books in underground libraries
along the highways of the Southwest. You are
lighting the fires of imagination in young minds
of all cultures along your route. You are
the most dangerous caravan in America.

Houston, San Antonio, El Paso, Las Cruces,
'Burque, and on to Tucson where the San Patricios
await you! Irishmen who fought for Mexicanos
in the Mexican American War now hover
like a ghost army over your caravan
to remind all people to learn, to share,
to love books like members of your own family.

Beware, Inquisitors of Arizona. Beware.
You are not welcome anywhere.
A caravan of *librotraficantes* is rolling
intellectual thunder your way. It is
the most dangerous caravan in America
on a mission to bring illegal wet books
to your students so they may see the world
through eyes clear, intelligent, and free.

Inquisitors of Arizona, you lock up books.
Inquisitors of Arizona, you invade the classroom.
Inquisitors of Arizona, you bully young students.
Inquisitors of Arizona, you missed the news:
Inquisitors went out of style centuries ago.

Books have been, are, always will be
illegal aliens, illegal immigrants, undocumented
ideas to light up the visions that make us human.

Inquisitors of Arizona and elsewhere:
First you ban cultures. Then you ban books.
Then you stoke the ovens to burn the books.
Then you stoke the ovens to burn the people
who love those books. But not this time.

Librotraficantes you are

the most dangerous caravan in America
the most dangerous caravan in America
the most dangerous caravan in America

02/18/12

Margaret Randall

I and *Am*

Kike, nigger, greaser, injun, chink,
slut, faggot, dyke: ugly words
bloated by fear and ignorance
strut the streets again these days,
greedy and shameless.

Meanwhile *I* and *am* huddle together,
hoping no one separates their fragile bodies.
Longer words take refuge in crowds,
confident numbers will keep them safe
or give them leverage.

Stormy always mentions weather,
the oldie that resonates.
She shies away from talk of climate change
or other complicated problems
on a map too gone for games.

We hear rumors of a renegade colony
where deceitful words
flood the market with counterfeit:
nation-building, melting pot, democracy,
historical revision and *natural disaster.*

And we resist. *I am. You are. We are,*
open our tired hearts,
retrieve those battered books,
welcome the brave words home,
let memory in.

Some insist: *Sticks and stones will break my bones*
but words will never hurt me:
Don't make me laugh. Or cry.

Banned words ban history, banned history
bans memory. Life withers and dies.

So *I* and *am* twin up for the long haul,
cling to each other in dignity,
victims of every injustice
beyond those hollow stand-ins
meant to bring us all down.

Ask your doctor if death is right for you.
Embed the modern reporter
in every lie poisoning our air
as it erases the stories
of who we were, and why.

For all those books that saved our lives,
the clandestine words are ready
to come out of hiding and nurture our children.
Let us tend the safe houses,
leave fresh water along the trail.

Andrea J. Serrano
Lament*
Burque, Nuevo Mexico, Aztlan

I want to write angry words about Arizona
fill up line after line of my notebook
with words like hate, ignorance, disbelief and fuck you
poetry filled with bravado
daring Arizona to pick a fight with me

I want to throw a finger at Arizona's villains
the culprits who wish to ban
our history
our books
our people

I want to pen a hateful masterpiece
but the words don't flow
my thoughts are muddled
my voice is frozen
as if Arizona's censoring hand
is gripping my throat
fingers wrapped tight
wanting me to remain silent about the war
that has been waged against my people

This poem is supposed to be about
the Tucson Unified School District's ban of Ethnic Studies
this poem is supposed to be lines of outrage over books
so subversive
they have been banned
Shakespeare, Zinn, Cisneros, Urrea, Alexie, Hooks
they were shoved into boxes
because they are
by
about

for
Brown people
all people
I can't describe what it felt like to be in the 11th grade
open my U.S. history book
and not find a single person who looked like me

this poem was meant to be angry
but instead
is bewildered, disgusted, shocked, hurt, sad
this poem is a very confused poet's lament over hate
specifically
hatred of Chicanos and Mexicanos
I don't understand why my people
like so many others
have been targets for violence
since the beginning of our existence

I am not a resident of Arizona
but borders and state lines do not exist
for Indigenous people
we are meant to walk wherever we wish
still, Arizona's influence
spills over to New Mexico
boils over to Texas
seeps into Birmingham
where four little girls
were martyred on September 15, 1963
because they were defenseless
because their lives were deemed worthless
because they were Black
I wait in fear
for four more to die
because they are Mexican
I wait in fear for another Brisenia Flores
a nine year old girl slaughtered in Arizona because
she was Mexican

I wonder why the President didn't attend her funeral
I wonder what her killers thought
when they looked into her eyes before ending her short life
I wonder why no one made a big deal about her murder
I wonder why the pro-life right didn't protect her

I want to shout my angriest words
but they don't come
maybe because they are being
shouted by the governors
and the tea partiers
the minute-men
and every day folks who have no idea why they hate Brown
        people
they just do
I have to pause
because shouting over ignorance
only sounds like more shouting

My words are scribbled in margins
and scrawled across the middle of the page
my throat may be gripped
my history may be banned
but it is not erased
and like the relentless sun beating down on the Arizona desert
we will not be ignored

---

*On May 30, 2009, Raul Flores (29) and his daughter Brisenia (9), were murdered during a home invasion in Arivaca, Arizona, by Shawna Forde and accomplices, who were members of MAD (Minutemen American Defense), a neo-Nazi group of border vigilantes. They robbed the family, wounding Gina Gonzalez (Raul's girlfriend) who survived by playing dead. The MAD group thought their victims were undocumented workers here illegally from from Mexico, but they were all native-born American citizens. Forde and her second-in-command, who has been linked to the White Supremicist Aryan Nations, were convicted and sentenced to death.

Tanaya Winder

In the Days of Banned Books

We've entered a New World
Order on words, days
of economic deprivation
where only one percent thrives.
Times dictated by greediness
and fear, days when books
are banned by the belief
consumed. Unnerved
from tainted verbs,
small pox blankets waiting
to infect them with brownness,
as if it seeps through pages
it's become contagious
to their white space.
The world changed
from childhood where I roamed
aisles, books stacked high
reaching for titles, birds to carry me
into other worlds. Lift me into flight.
Destination: past. Remember
though we've been tortured, raped,
and burned, we always come back.
Even when they try to silence cries
the classroom caged bird still sounds a song.
Didn't we first start losing ourselves
with tongues banished?
If we bury all books containing
atrocity will that change
history? This has happened before.
If history repeats itself
I worry about the children I have
yet to have: will I be able to read to them
in bed at night? Will they wake up asking:

where are the books? where are the books?
What happened to them? What will I read
my children? And where?
Classroom banished words
become contraband. So I will
put bird ready-messengers
to paper, hold my piece
in my mouth until words
migrate out. Though their wings may ache
with oppression, they'll recite oral histories
hidden in the constellations,
we will tell our children
we needed the entire sky
to tell our story
the blank page
just wasn't
enough
space

assemblage sculpture by William Georgenes

Bruce Holsapple
Sense of Arrest

Out back the first A beams,
the roof started, never
set into place, a stack of 2 by 6s,
sheets of plywood, gutter pipes
ready to go—Only one window in
but the rest stored under
the floor, the door open—
a food bin with canned meat,
vegetables, plastic box of
books, H.P. Lovecraft, classic Zen texts,
Whitehead's *Interpretation of Science*
tools left about, hammer, saw
a case of bottled water

The grayed floor ruined by sun, rain
the roughened walls, rolls of insulation
& more lumber under a tattered
plastic tent, tent ribs collapsed
trash bin broke open

A trail down the hillside
where he or she carried
that lumber up, lugged concrete
foundation blocks, cast iron stove,
all the building gear, all
one trip at a time
must have taken a month, two months
left on an instant—

A family emergency, perhaps
They meant to come back
or hadn't quite figured
what to do, but needed to get away

So obviously a spiritual enterprise
That's what the books said,

what the location said—
desert hilltop, sandy view
Not failure so much as
the sense of arrest

of abandon, didn't quite know
what they had singled out to accomplish

look up thru the rafters
the unfinished roof
gray plywood sides, rainy sky
lightning flash

bird nesting above the door frame
young birds calling

Bruce Holsapple

[untitled]

Paddling a small green kayak
south from the Cambridge Road
down a branch of the Sebasticook
in Maine, weeks of rain
the river high enough
that I slide over log jams,
sluice thru the ledge shoals
above pebbled sandbars,
to where it enters low farm land
begins to enlarge, beaver dams
cranberry bogs, deeper & slow
prior fir & hemlock become leafy maples
that's why almost no one
goes there, too swampy to navigate
& has been left, thick shrubs,
sedge, cattails, green embankment
mire & mosquitoes

I once camped, 16 years old
in an abandoned sugaring shack
above this swamp, all but fallen apart
full of porcupine duff
to prove to my dad
I could live alone, but hadn't
even packed food enough
lasted a week

Encouraged by that high water,
paddling upstream a day later
almost to the North Dexter bridge
the swampy trough regress
into rocky shallows, rapids
a wild stream deep in the woods
practically unrecognizable
save for beaver dams at Snow Brook
several flooded acres of alder

I mean from where it starts
barely larger than a brook
youth & age, as it were

& the isolation I felt on both trips—
that was a big part of why I went,
to get alone with myself—
an odd doubling phrase, isn't it?
It's struggle that does that
me & the kayak, the kayak
& the stream, the stream now
versus then—how one then can
"make something" of one's self—
respond to a challenge
one on one, narrowing
to the point of contact

Bruce Holsapple
[untitled]

18 miles from town & no telephone
a long drive, dirt roads
such that when you're out here, you need learn
what's ahead, say if the power goes
as it does with storms
no electricity: no pump & often
no heat, so at the least you'll want
candles, water, thermal blankets
for there's too much that
goes seriously wrong—
the car broken down
dead battery, flat tire
not to think thru matches, food,
sources of water
Or not emergencies
so much as think actions thru
learn what you depend on, the scaffold
by which you resurrect yourself
each day—

learn what your predecessors
contended with
how their attitudes formed
the way it works out here

think if you had to haul water
chop wood to stay alive
protect sheep, nurse corn

shit & all you've got to do
is get to work on time—
it's laid out like an assembly line
nothing thoughtful at all

Bruce Holsapple
[untitled]

Making love with X on the dunes
surf crashing, loud black wind
but then a cop stumbles up, flashlight glaring
saying what, that we'd trespassed?
he'd spotted our car & afterwards
she's furious! in turn insulting me,
so that we fight driving back to her parent's
Why'd he come after us?
that's what she was mad about—
or what she *said* she was angry with
Those beaches are public
No, that's right, there was a curfew
but I think she was ashamed
a respectable girl—that's
what she covered up
making love on a public beach—
what she'd surrendered to
& when a policeman crashed thru that
with his spotlight, she turned on me
as somehow causing our vulnerability
Am I just now making this up?
A shift in priorities, for sure!
I still hear that wind, startle
at the glare, but wouldn't have
recalled the moment, that wind—
if he hadn't, if she hadn't
abruptly turned on me

Tanaya Winder
The Weight of Water

I.

When I first arrived into this world, I flew
on ancient winds. I was born into a creation story.

II.

Long ago, my great great great grandmother met her other half.
He, too, flew on winds, then as one of many
grains of sand – each, split in half looking
        for the other. Back then, humans were only spirits

searching for connections. *Long ago,* a single grain found
another, my grandmother. So, they asked the Creator
for bodies, to know what it was like to touch each other.
They did and foresaw their child would die in birth.
        So they prayed – *Save her,* each sacrificing

something in return. The man entered the spirit world
as a horse and the woman opened herself up
from the center to give him a piece of her
        to remain connected.

III.

In the middle of the desert
there is a lake created out of tears. *Long ago*
there was a mother with four daughters:
North, East, South, and West. Once they grew up
each daughter left to follow her own direction.

Saddened by this loss, the mother cried
so intensely the skies envied her ability to create
such moisture. Days turned to months, months to
years and tears gathered in salty pools that gravitated
towards each other's weight. Unable to release
her bitterness, the mother turned to stone.

221

Today, the Stone Mother waits
Come back to me my children.
Come back to me.

IV.

I spent my childhood floating
on my back, steady in between,
      the sky, sun, moon –

all of creation above me
and the lake, beneath. There is a peace
      in being carried by waves.

V.

How much we do not let go of
when we carry the weight of water,
      the tears around us, in a generation

out of balance. We carry Stone
Mother's cries, *come back to me* in our hair
      thick enough to clog drains and water rises.

I dream spirits swim in the Milky Way,
rallying the stars in a call to arms. Shake us
out of silence so we can hear the cries to:
      come back, come back, come back.

Charles Trumbull

Gleaners: Romania, 1990

A morning dark and cold:
The harvest now long past,
The oily scythes rehung,
What grain there was is ground.

Long shadows cast by cut-off stalks,
Grim stripes across the frosted field,
White and gray-an old man's cheek,
Pale and ready for dying.

The barren village women come
              (They are the truly needy);
And now the rich ones flock here too
              (They speak of thrift and saving),
Too glad to pay the peasant folk
              (Who call it economic)
To scrabble for the overlooked,
Neglected, and forgotten.

The children are the germ of love
In this, a fertile land laid bare.
Likewise are they the seed of famine.

Charles Trumbull
Operating Instructions

Congratulations on your purchase!
Used prudently and with proper care
Your Snagger™ Dreamcatcher
Could last a lifetime.

The Snagger™ Dreamcatcher
Can be employed in your home
Anywhere that dreams occur:
Living room or kitchen,
Patio or closet;
But it has proven most popular
In the bedroom.

Our innovative patented
ConstantStrain® technology
Decisively isolates
Good dreams from bad.
Cauchemars and incautious thoughts
Are securely caught and cached
In the silken webbing.
Any accumulated
Grimy sludge normally dissipates
In bright sun and fresh air
Every morning.

Be sure to hang your Snagger™
Opposite a dedicated aperture
Where fugitive visions
Can vent. Should your hole attract
Waxy buildup, sclerosis, or congestion,
Vigorous scrubbing with a stiff brush
Usually restores proper channeling .

After installation and activation
Of your Snagger™ Dreamcatcher
You should be careful to maintain

A proper distance from the device.
Sometimes, during warm spells,
The Snagger™ has been known
To drain a careless dreamer completely
Dry of doubts, and even hopes,
In a very short time.

In case of psychic malfunction
Your Snagger™ may have to be
Uninstalled. Please dispose
Of a decommissioned Dreamcatcher
In a responsible manner.

Richard Wolfson

Where Memories Sleep

Once we were incapable of escaping promises,
our ears lost in never-ending fire-history,
the dried talon of disappointment, clipped to our collars
with ashen recollection of a time of grace.

The fervor of a clandestine retirement
tied like a bell, witnessing penance,
song of nonchalance, lacking time remorse,
the ancients foretold this chapter of cyber cathedral;

when stones smash against the eyes of the wind,
gnashing heard just beyond nebula notation
at insistence of the tape that measures memories,
drop of first snowflake, like a magnetic detective.

The snake of where the past is hidden,
coils like the smile on the back of a mirror.

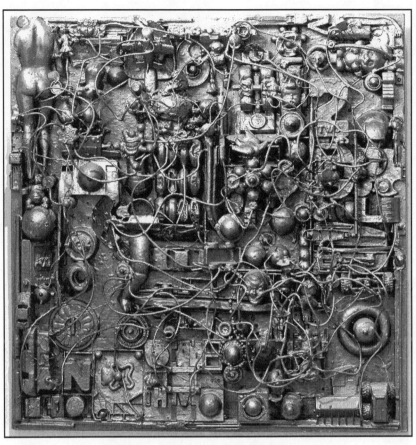

assemblage sculpture by William Georgenes

Introducing María Vázquez Valdéz

She is in the ruins at Petra, Jordan, a camera lifted to her eye. She is sleeping in a makeshift tent on Mexico City's Reforma Avenue along with thousands of others protesting yet another fabricated outcome to her country's presidential election. She is standing on Plateau Point, the high thrust of land deep in Grand Canyon, listening to the power of the Colorado River as it roars through Hance Rapid. On stage in the University of Mexico's impressive *aula magna*, a brilliant orange shawl flows from her slender body. Wherever she is, poetry moves through María Vázquez Valdéz as if it were on its home map.

María was born in Zacatecas, Mexico, one 24th of January some four decades ago. She lives in Mexico City where she works as a journalist, photographer, translator, editor of art and architectural books, and as her deepest self, which is as a poet. María is a weaver of life as well as of words. She has traveled the world— from India to Peru—experiencing moments of deadly menace and exquisite beauty, many of which have found their way into her rich and evocative poetry. She practices yoga. She meditates.

María did her undergraduate work in journalism and communication at the UNAM (National Autonomous University of Mexico), and later obtained a Masters in book editing. She is currently the editor-in-chief of an important arts magazine out of Zacatecas called *Arcilla roja* (Red Clay).

I first came in contact with María a decade ago, when she was preparing her seminal anthology *Voces desdobladas/ Unfolded Voices*, bilingual selections of poetry and interviews with several Mexican and U.S. women poets, of whom I was one.

228

Over the next few years we would translate one another's work, appear in a number of readings together, and become fast friends. Among her other publications are *Estancias* (2004), a collection of cultural essays; *Rayuela de museos* (2005), a large volume about the world's most important art museums, text and photos by the author; and *Caldero* (1999) and *Estaciones del albatros* (2008), both poetry books.

The following is a very small sampling of María's poetry, a taste I hope will leave the reader wanting more.

—Margaret Randall

Flight

I have journeyed to beauty's circumference
to the place where the clear deep
river of life is born

Configuration of all things shifted in fractals
and unknown worlds revealed themselves,
brilliant hymns,
      deep drums,
      dancing fireflies

It is all there
and I didn't see it
until I removed myself
so it could exist

Then the miracle occurred:
I sprouted wings,
           salmon pink reached those heights
after all the storms.

The caterpillar saw light at last,
and was surprised by its taste,
and the butterfly danced
with earth's pulse,
describing infinite images
of incalculable brilliance.

---

translation by Margaret Randall

Coagulated Blood

To the little girls of Oventic

I

That morning fog
is a sigh,
a moist secret

A blue flame
glinting in the women's eyes
in the eyes of the men

Chiapas,
a fertile field
of green giants,
ladders decorated
with shiny ribbons
and bruised flesh

II

A little girl
climbs the frozen hill

From above she sees
a tide of soldiers
chopping the bodies
as if they were trees,
they hold
her silenced
empty heart
between their boots

Farther up
she knows
the brutal
blood-letting

The red trunks
of the Ceiba
are stumps now,
broken too,
uprooted

III

In a room
made of mud and wood
an old man dies

His feet are tracks
sewn of open wounds,
from this deaf land
his flesh was exiled
to the highlands

His shadow dances in the dark,
cut by the scissors
of a single candle

It calls forth the ancient ones
who own the wind,
the red jaguars
who follow the rains
and rivers

It calls for the spirit
embroidered by Moon,
a lonely memory
dying in the swamps
like his descendents

IV

Chiapas,
luminous
as the flowering zinacantec
that surrounded by such green
lets its sparkle drop,
like the cleanly adorned tzeltal
that gazes profound and sad,
like the tzotzil suspended in midair
at the highest reach of mountain,
beaten by wool and cold

Upon what knife edge
do you harvest life?

Broken in the folds of the earth,
a defenseless woman surrounded by beasts,
your womb plundered in the thorns

Chiapas,
brilliant reflection
in eyes and lakes,
land darkened
by coagulated blood,
woman graceful
as fire,
as water.

———
translation by Margaret Randall

One

because nothing matters
neither sunflower nor that brown bird
pyramid nor tree

you get smaller on the wind
nothing matters in this silence

the old man speaks from his high seat
he says your eyes do not see:
everything is Maya the Vedanta says,
mirage in movement

nothing matters
neither years nor the dust
that wakes in our lungs

fingers tumbling through mist
in search of dreams

nothing matters between you and me
and an ancient spiral unwinds
it brings you to my hands
fresh water and pedestal
luminous quartz in my belly
and white flowers through the smoke nothing matters

running in decapitated rivers
life scatters and reaches
perfect peaks
of eagles and the breath of altitude

from there to the deepest chasm nothing matters
everything finds a new sun, a dazzling moon
or hell

but nothing matters

nothing matters because all is one,
a single drumbeat
under the sky
deep heartbeat that wakes
from sleep or agony

ecstasy or anguish
it's the same runaway colt in your breast

nothing matters not you not me not anyone

because all is one

---

translation by Margaret Randall

Don Russ
A Taos Raven

Thoughts on a Block Print by the artist Mieshiel

Raven has swallowed
        three large stars and – as filled, as still,
        as he is, fitted into a night-sky's page
        of twinkling signs – sits cloaked

        in wings, his eyes unchanging mirror
        of a changing moon. Whatever is to know
        I say he knows so I – another son
        of heaven's dust – know too.

        In words I choose for both of us
        I frame the dream of life, a spell of love,
and – for me at least – a paper stay
        against the end of days.

Morning Wings

 In my hallway a feather
of autumn sunshine has fallen, still
trembles separate from the rest

of day. And pausing between
my empty bedroom and the settling
clutter of my desk, I poke it

with my toe: all my shutters
closed, my tree leafed dead, yet sky
comes through,

this moment the local
habitation of all there is, my life
this flight in place.

Judith Toler

The Four Seasons of Crow

summer

I open the garage door
the car isn't there

I look under the doormat
the cardboard boxes

I look in the driveway
up and down the street

I look beneath the bushes
then up to the highest branches

where I find my car sitting
between two black crows

fall

fourteen crows
puff up their feathers
pretend to be ravens
fall upon me

I try throwing stones
at them, they laugh
krawk krawk krawk
flap wings against fat bellies

I throw skillets at them
a crockpot, a bottle of ketchup
my sofa, the kitchen sink
they laugh harder and harder

winter

a murder of crows
black against white snow
my house is empty
there is nothing
left to throw
except myself

spring

I loosen my arms
wheeling into spirals
black wings slanted white in sun
round bone, hollow eye
rising iridescence
all of us
all of us flying

Steven Martínez
Converging, Shimmer

there is another path
to my grandmother's graveyard
it lengthens through the sway
of a swath of stray marigold
past a blind mole's entrance
in morning moon silver

raw wind
and a twinge of nostalgia
meet a rough turn of rock
upsets rested frost
bald step, scrape a limb
knock a curse-word loose
from her lips sometimes
then a hug, or red jam
on two hands of bread

here hot breath is annexed to crickets
whose ruckus crescendos in the bowl
of a cliff-base, filled with the scuffle
of faraway aspen, leaves flame out

shedding my jacket, down in the dust
to hear her grave-song launder between us
      mellow, crimson in my mouth
as sunrise sifts to whispering gravesites

the other path reveals itself crawling
to the highway, the grid, the unnamed
suits of the city, dark, ill-fitted to the wind
she knew best, and lodged in my chest
the knots begin easing, a fluttering
affirmation between clasped hands—
her song I glean in the spark of a cardinal
with newborn wings, beginning to spread.

Tani Arness

White Feathers

The two-foot snowy owl
     Nyctea scandiaca
like scrimshawed ivory—
hunts by day,
the ground covered in snow.

White feathers fall from sky
     (ice)
The people
     (village)
know what is coming—
the thick curves of spring.

With a nest built shallow on the ground,
the owl hears the sound of a vole
running a tunnel beneath snow;
he performs a stiff courtship dance
with the vole in the grip of his talon.

In spring, smooth needles of ice
burst into prisms
edging sun.
The round of the world brings gifts.

Tani Arness

Tower of Babel

Genesis 11

We were building a staircase to heaven,
a square base with sloping, stepped sides leading upward.
(Who hasn't wanted such a ladder?)
But the Lord said,
Then nothing they plan
will be impossible for them. . .
and he pulled it down.

The whole world had one language;
we spoke moon and antelope, stars and rivers—
and then there was a confusion of strange
vowels and clickings on our tongues—
we spoke without hearing words.

The Lord scattered us
over the earth
and we stopped building
towers to God,
and we started building
roads back to each other.
Lovers, unable to silence their desire,
whispered sweet nothings, rolling R's and swooning vowels,
into each other's ears,
and another language was born of lips and tongue.

I, too, wanted to find what was invisible,
that place where nothing is impossible.
I, too, baked bricks in the sun,
fastened them together with tar,
carefully placed each piece beneath heaven, constructing my
      destiny.
And I watched as God scattered it all.

Perhaps destiny is not the right word,

and ambition is not from God.
Maybe there is something better to build than towers.
Maybe only language overcomes separation
even between heaven and earth.
Perhaps words are meant to be indecipherable prayers,
and God is just the wind.
Scattered. God scattered our hearts.

Ned Dougherty
She Is Easily Missed

I.

god lives softly somewhere in a hogan
She wakes and sweeps her circle clean of mouse turds every
      morning
fry bread and honey breakfast
it would never seem like She has anything in her cupboards
or enough wood to last the winter

She drives a green pick up with white trim
She speeds
rolls her cigarette one handed and navigates with a knee

climbs the same cliff at noon each day
calms the desert temperatures with lullabies

She has named every pebble on her land
sees a bit of herself in each one

She drums at all the powwows

She plays bingo every tuesday

visits the same gas station
orders black coffee and drinks from a styrofoam cup

She never misses the local basketball games
girls or boys
can remember all their stats and team records
dating back to the sixties

and even if they never shot a ball through a hoop
She knows every child's name
everyone knows She loves the children

II.

recently god's lover left her
the other could not live so simply
in so much silence

lover told their friends of god's unending love
made everyone believe She had a plan for her people
but really She kept retreating

when they were out together
lover would speak for her
and get it all wrong

quietly in bed She would tell lover
most opinions of her were well off base
lover would turn her back and She would find the couch

lover made up words for her like omniscient and omnipotent
but the people began to fear her

they blamed her for their scrawny livestock in drought years
hollow wallets
and their kids with pneumonia

She never blamed lover's boasts or fevered zeal
her love never waned
She loves her even in distance

III.

long ago She bore a son
She swelled then shrunk
and found her purpose shaping man

the boy always sat with the elders
they sought his maturing wisdom

the government sent this only son to vietnam
his mother grayed and wrinkled around squinted eyes

She bought sheep when they shipped him off
cared for them as best as anyone could
considering the clay of desert in their graze

the people called her good shepherd
because in desolation
She only lost one
and has dog tags to remember

IV.

to find god
look for the woman alone
racing down 491 in her truck
or purchasing Budweiser on game day
She is easily missed

The Crystal Prism of Poetry:
Harvena Richter (1917-2011)

by Jon Knudsen

In 1928 novelist Conrad Richter, with his wife and child, stepped down from the train into the Albuquerque sunshine. Like many others departing the train that day, one of them was coughing. His wife had tuberculosis. His daughter Harvena was eleven years old. They had left their beloved Pine Tree Farm in Pennsylvania and moved to New Mexico looking to ease his wife's suffering and perhaps find a cure.

Harvena's father was extremely busy trying to support his family selling short stories to magazines . . . and it only got more difficult as the Great Depression set in and the markets dried up. Harvena went to school. Her mother coped as best she could. Her father sold stories for very little money to pulp magazines. These times are documented in the very readable and fascinating Richter biography, **Conrad Richter: A Writer's Life,** written by David R. Johnson. Later, Harvena published her father's journals with a slightly different and telling twist, **Writing to Survive: The Private Notebooks of Conrad Richter.**

Things eventually got better for the Richters. His popular novel **Sea of Grass** was published in 1937 and made into a movie a decade later. In 1951 he won the Pulitzer Prize for Fiction.

Financial success allowed Harvena to do what any young writer would want to do if her father had just won the Pulitzer Prize for Fiction: she left for New York. She worked writing advertising copy for several New York fashion houses and she toured Europe. In 1956 she rode a Vespa motor scooter from Genoa, Italy to Tehran, Persia – later publishing a fictionalized account of the trip called **Passage to Teheran.**

Harvena eventually moved back to Albuquerque, living in a rambling adobe in the north valley for 40 years until her death in July of last year at the age of 94.

The Richter Family, circa 1950

The following poems are from two of her books of poetry, **The Innocent Island** and **Frozen Light: The Crystal Poems**.

The title **The Innocent Island** refers to Pine Tree Farm. But of course it is more than that. It is her elementary school years and childhood itself. It is that period in her life before her mother got sick and her father famous. It is the world before the Great Depression. And most importantly, it represents a very secure place where nothing ever changes.

247

Her poems are rarely just a revisiting of childhood moments. There is something to be found there for her as an adult. Something worth searching for.

Her poetry is not conversational in tone. It is modern, but certainly not 21st century in its construction, many times extending an image as far as possible. In "The Island" she remembers her farm while holding an egg in a beautiful eleven line riff that just gets better and better.

> Sin was no question—everything was whole,
> whole as the egg whose shell need not be broken
> to know what lies inside.
> I palmed that egg, and tipped it back and forth
> to feel its yellow sun now rise, now set,
> a hidden island in an inland sea.
> My eye became that island, yolked in blue:
> it swung full circle, missed no sail or fin.
> Like a space mariner I reeled from world to world—
> each tree, or rock, or flower became an earth:
> each was miraculous, each cradled all.

She was pretty much left to her own devices on the farm, exploring and wandering the fields and forests. The magical "Corn Mother" takes us from the planting season to the winter fields. But it is not about the corn—it is about the girl.

> In whistling shade I stuck a foot
> storklike as theirs into the earth.
> I could have taken root, and grown
> as thin as a green pipe, and known
> the sun lie hot upon my leaves
> and felt the gripes of greening birth.

Perhaps the most haunting of all the poems in **The Innocent Island** is called "Meeting." The metaphysical reversal of time and roles is just stunning. It begins with the straightforward line

> I see myself as a child.

and walks the reader through the farm to this:

> It is she now who is real,
> and I the ghost of her future,
> the specter she will meet
> at the road's turning.

Her book **Frozen Light: The Crystal Poems** is an interesting series of short pieces that are themselves gemstones. Crisp and hard-edged on the outside, they are in fact translucent looks into several different worlds . . . the worlds of ideas, of personhood, of heart. Each crystal has its own characteristics, and their molecular latticework serves up a variety of surprising discoveries. Take the poem "Flaw," for example. Its simple statement on the outside belies the level of meaning on the inside. So elegant. So short. So deep. So matter-of-factly true.

> **XVI Flaw**
> The crystal's no
> apologist—
> "I have a flaw,"
> it says, and then
> goes on to shield
> the nasty spot
> with a great show
> of glittering light.

That piece could have had some politicians in mind.

A personal favorite of the crystal poems is "Crystal as Temple," a piece that traces the ironies and historical connections of crystalline architecture from Egyptians to modern churches.

A knowledge of gems and geology, however, is not something she expects from the reader. As she states in the forward to the book, "I have used only a fraction of the terminology, and very little of the esoteric lore of the crystal, which takes in energy fields and healing properties. These paths I leave to the reader to pursue."

*Harvena Richter
in 2008*

The Island

Five years on a farm that scarcely was a farm–
no animals or fowl inside the barn,
no butcherings. I never even knew
the common barnyard matings.
I made my own mythologies of land and beast,
how spirits lived in every bush and tree,
how creature brought forth creature magically.
O innocent island, ringed with innocence,
it might have risen straight up from the sea
with seventy swans singing.
Sin was no question–everything was whole,
whole as the egg whose shell need not be broken
to know what lies inside.
I palmed that egg, and tipped it back and forth
to feel its yellow sun now rise, now set,
a hidden island in an inland sea.
My eye became that island, yolked in blue:
it swung full circle, missed no sail or fin.
Like a space mariner I reeled from world to world–
each tree, or rock, or flower became an earth:
each was miraculous, each cradled all.

Meeting

I see myself as a child.

I have just come back to the farm—
another family lives there.
I move in a mist across
the log bridge, up the lane
where the bittersweet used to hang,
and the chicken grapes.
The old barn holds horses now,
the house has grown,
the woodshed is not there.

I follow the invisible path
past the rhubarb patch
and suddenly see her:
her hair is pulled back,
a single barrette clamps it,
she is wearing
her father's old felt hat.

She turns as if she knows
and gives me a level glance.
She wishes me to go—
I disturb the full sense of her life.
She feels a cold wind blow.

It is she now who is real,
and I the ghost of her future,
the specter she will meet
at the road's turning.

Burrs

I can't pull them out,
those burrs that stick
in the mind,
that burrow like ticks,
those barbed
beggar lice
from childhood.

How else do I pick up
in my dreams
Indian fires raging
in these woods?

Or a signal
flashed to me
across the field
from a child picking
wild strawberries
fifty years ago?

Corn Mother

I was a child who roamed the farm
without a creature of my kind—
alone I filled my empty world
with what my restless wit could find:
familiars filched from wood and field,
from stalk and flower, bush and tree.
And when my fancies wearied me
I tagged the hired man on his round,
rode the plough horses, rode the drag
that swam the furrows like a boat,
followed the farmer as he sowed
dropping in four grains to the hole,
hoeing them over down the row
and muttering to the summer wind:
one for the cutworm, one for the crow,
one to rot, and one to grow.

That was the ritual which began
the magic of my greening year,
waiting for young shoots to appear
from that small wrinkled gold below
that seemed as hard and dry as stone.
I felt the magic in my bones
the while I watched that rising corn
whose mysteries I did not know
but saw them springing in the sun.
Corn kin they were in essence then,
companions down those long green halls
where narrow-limbed their living walls
were sprung from earth as I had been,
their roots curved like a rooster's toes—
a grip on life I knew full well—
and heads that read the rain and sky.
Their tops grew taller far than I
in those long weeks of hot July,

and frost would nearly brown the hill
before the ears were thick and full
and yellow as a chicken's bill.
Those long green weeks I tracked the halls
with paper cracklings all around
the green pitch of a growing sound.
I ran my hand along the stalks
as slick as brass rods on my bed;
my fingers found the jointed grooves,
and felt the white milk run within;
and cradled in a crook of stem
the child of grain in swaddled green.
In whistling shade I stuck a foot
storklike as theirs into the earth.
I could have taken root, and grown
as thin as a green pipe, and known
the sun lie hot upon my leaves
and felt the gripes of greening birth.

September went; October found
the husked ears in a pyramid
of pebbled gold upon the ground.
The corn had gone; the barren shocks
were teepees of a vanished race.
One morning saw the fields lie bare,
but on the far hills, mists of smoke
suggested someone camping there
who might be back another year
to fill that deep and empty place.

IV The Seed

An accident?
or was the seed
implanted when the earth
   was without form,
a shaft of light
   cowering in chaos,
and then
that sudden birth
out of a crazy nest of gneiss–
the crystal?

Who can tell
the shape of things unborn,
waiting for some word,
some propulsion
   into dawn?

VII Geode

A roundish rock
light and hollow;
you crack it open
like a nut
and find inside
a sight to startle:
pinnacles and towers
of bristling crystal,
amethyst, jasper,
chalcedony, quartz—
a hidden city
rayed with light,
a purse laden
with lustrous coin,
the inner kingdom
the heart searches.

XII Twinned Crystals

Some crystals have
a doppelgänger,
a mirror twin
joined hip to shoulder,
identity doubled
like the twin you
always yearned for,
that knew your thoughts,
that spoke your words.
The crystal twin
is the other half,
the hidden captain,
the gold ghost
who walks beside you
whom no one knows.

XVI Flaw

The crystal's no
apologist—
"I have a flaw,"
it says, and then
goes on to shield
the nasty spot
with a great show
of glittering light.

XXII Crystal as Temple

Whatever architect
contrived the crystal—
plotted the angles,
cleaved the planes,
laid out the axes of
prisms, rhombohedrons,
capped the pyramids
with perfect
terminated points—
he hid them in
a river bed,
a volcano's craw,
a hollow place,
a deep vein running
like silver in the earth.
Finding them
is to discover
a secret temple
in the woods—
an exquisite theorem
whose geometry
was copied by Egyptians,
borrowed by Greeks,
adapted to any
vaulted church
or chapel where
worshippers convene
to clear
their essence,
let the light
sift through.

Contributors

David Abel is a poet, editor, bookseller, and teacher in Portland, Oregon. He is the author of several chapbooks and artist's books, and a new collection of poems, **Float**, is imminent from Chax Press. One of the founders of the Spare Room reading series, now in its eleventh year, he is also a research fellow of the Center for Art + Environment of the Nevada Museum of Art, and is co-administering 13 Hats, a collaborative platform for ten Portland writers and visual artists. He is Gene Frumkin's literary executor.

William Allen, Jr., of Los Angeles, has been involved in many aspects of the Arts, holds undergraduate and graduate degress from USC and UCLA, as well as the Inner City Cultural Arts Institute. He has taught theater and dance and participated in both. He was a guest dancer with the Bill T. Jones Dance Company in a production of "Last Supper at Uncle Tom's Cabin"; with the Dance Theater of Harlem; and the Alvin Ailey company. He was dancer/choreographer for the 20th Century Fox Studios's "Tribute to Lena Horne" and a dancer for a production of "Tribute to the Black Woman" by the Trina Parks Company, which included Nancy Wilson, Eartha Kitt, Sidney Poitier, Roscoe Lee Brown, Dr. Maya Angelou, Nona Hendryx, Stevie Wonder, Chaka Khan and Bill Withers. His literary endeavors include prose, poetry, and theater. He performed in a production of his own play "The Sun/Son can shine" (Skylight Theater, 2011) and has been involved with spoken word productions with the Lambda Literary Foundation (2012). His poetry has appeared in various publications, and a short story was recently published in an anthology, *Tapestries of Faith*.

Cathy Arellano – In December 2011, her poem "Coyolxauqui," a modern telling of an old story, was published in *Turtle Island to Abya Yala: A Love Anthology of Art and Poetry by Native American and Latina Women*. Her work has also been published in anthologies (*Chicana Lesbians: The Girls Our Mothers Warned Us About* and *Days I Moved Through Ordinary Sounds: The Teachers of WritersCorps in Poetry and Prose)*; journals; newspapers; and blogs. Her chapbook, **I Love My Women, Sometimes They Love Me**, is full of broken-hearted lesbian love poems suitable for queer or straight folks who have loved, been loved, or been left. She teaches Developmental English full-time at Central New Mexico Community College; part-time with University of New Mexico's Chicana and Chicano Studies Program; and workshops in the community. She has just started her own blog called Life in the Bleachers (lifeinthebleachers. blogspot.com).

Tani Arness currently loves living and teaching in beautiful Albuquerque, NM. She earned her Master's degree in Creative Writing from the University of New Mexico and has been published in numerous literary magazines including *Red Rock Review*, *Rhino*, *Santa Clara Review*, *Green Mountains Review* and *North American Review*.

Jabari Asad – Raised in the suburbs of Philadelphia, Jabari Asad began writing in high school. He started out writing love songs by imitating artists such as Gerald Levert. It wasn't until attending college at Lincoln University that he found his voice as a poet. After being exposed to the spoken word community at an on-campus open mic, he found his true passion. Embracing freedom from rhyme schemes and political correctness, he found a way to express himself without any limits. Jabari began doing open mics in Philadelphia in 2002 and performed at his first poetry slam in 2006 after moving to St. Louis. He returned to Philadelphia in 2007 and became an active member in The Fuze, Philadelphia's first official poetry slam venue. He performs at poetry slams and open mics throughout the city. Beyond poetry, Jabari works with youth in Camden and South Jersey, where he now resides.

Hakim Bellamy was given the tremendous honor of being selected in 2012 as the City of Albuquerque's first Poet Laureate. A national and regional Poetry Slam Champion, Bellamy holds three consecutive collegiate poetry slam titles at the University of New Mexico and two City Slam Champion titles in Albuquerque (2005) and Silver City, NM (2008). His poetry has been published in Albuquerque city buses and numerous anthologies. Bellamy was recognized as an honorable mention for the University of New Mexico Paul Bartlett Ré Peace Prize for his work as a community organizer and journalist and was recently bestowed the populist honor of "Best Poet" by *Local iQ* ("Smart List" 2010, 2011 & 2012) and *Alibi* ("Best of Burque" 2010, 2011 & 2012). He is the co-creator (with Carlos Contreras & Colin Diles Hazelbaker) of the multimedia Hip Hop theater production "Urban Verbs: Hip-Hop Conservatory & Theater" that has been staged throughout the country. He facilitates youth writing workshops for schools and community organizations in New Mexico and beyond. Hakim is currently finishing his MA in the Communications and Journalism Department at UNM. He is the proud father of a 4 year-old miracle and works as the Strategic Communication Director at Media Literacy Project.

John S. Blake has his first full collection of poems, **Beautifully Flawed,** in the pipeline by way of Urban Publishing (NYC). He's also about to publish his first in a series of memoir writings, "Wildflower – A Man Remembers a Remarkable Woman." His work has been accepted by *Two Bridges Review, InTheFray Magazine, Naugatuck River Review of Narrative Poetry, In The Biblical Sense Anthology, Sparrow Anthology,* and many other literary collections. He teaches poetry to teens nationwide as means to successfully overcome adversity.

Debbi Brody conducts poetry workshops and readings through out the Southwest. Her work has appeared in the *Santa Fe Literary Review, Sin Fronteras, Broomweed Journal, Poetica* and many other literary journals as well as numerous anthologies of note. She enjoys hearing from her readers through email at artqueen58@aol.com.

Gary L. Brower, who has taught at various universities, published three volumes of poetry and a CD in the last five years. He is one of the directors of the Duende Poetry Series of Placitas, NM, where he lives. Publications for 2012 include *In Paradise We Will Become Music* (poetry CD), and **Leaving Cairo, As If It Were A Dream** (a collaboration of poetry with photos and CD).

Álvaro Cardona-Hine is a poet, painter, composer, and all-around artist who lives in Truchas, New Mexico, where his gallery is located. Born in Costa Rica, he has lived in the U.S. since 1939, and has published some seventeen books of poetry, prose, and translations. Most recently, he published a book of poems with the late poet Gene Frumkin, **The Curvature of the Earth** (UNM Press, 2007), and a book of poems in Spanish, *Sucursal de Estrella* (UNM Press, 2006).

Hannah Craig lives in Pittsburgh, PA. Her work has recently appeared in the *American Literary Review, Columbia Review, 32Poems,* and elsewhere.

Jasmine Cuffee — A native of Albuquerque's South Valley, Cuffee has been active in the Albuquerque arts community for nearly 10 years. She was a member of the 2004 Poetry Slam team, 2005 Youth Poetry Champion, and 2007 City Slam Champion. As a performance poet and slam poetry champion, Jasmine has led numerous writing workshops and performances throughout New Mexico and the Western U.S. She has appeared in the *Bigger Boat Anthology, Earthships: A New Mecca Poetry Anthology,* and *¿De Veras?.* She is currently working on her first manuscript **Where the Arroyos and Train Tracks Meet,** which will follow her first chapbook, **Sunshine and Rapture**, released in 2007.

Ned Dougherty is a teacher, bartender and poet living in Taos, NM. His work has been published by several small presses across New Mexico and on the Internet. He is an active participant in the Taos poetry scene, hosting events, performing at readings, and cultivating the youth voice. Find his poetry at transplantedpoet.blogspot.com.

Janet Eigner, a Santa Fe-based dance writer, celebrates daily pleasures and hands-on work with nature, family, friends, social justice, and the joy of weekly poetry groups, one for 20 years, one for 10! From her chapbook, **Cornstalk Mother** (Puddinghouse), "Isaac's Blessing" is forthcoming in April 2012 on the Poetry Foundation website, *American Life in Poetry.* Selected publications: *American Life in Poetry; Adobe Walls, Blue Mesa, Drumbeat Review, Echoes, Hawaii Review, Manzanita, Mudfish, New Mexico Poetry Review, Visions International, Dance Magazine, Post Dispatch, New Mexican, The Reporter.*

Esther Feske is a book designer and artist in several media. She designed dozens of books for Penfield Books including the award-winning **Scandinavian Proverbs**, all her calligraphy and illustration. A cookbook she edited, designed and illustrated, **License to Cook New Mexico Style**, is a Penfield best-seller for 20 years. **Mexican Proverbs /**

Proverbios Mexicanos, which she edited and designed, was released in 2011.

Dr. Doris Fields is a poet, visual artist, and performance artist who has written two books of poetry and illustrated Phyllis Hotch's **A Little Book of Lies**. She has read her work throughout New Mexico and in Colorado, Georgia, New York, California, the Caribbean, and South Africa. Currently she serves as adjunct faculty at the University of New Mexico and at New Mexico Highlands University. Her research area is Intercultural Communication Competence. She lives in Placitas with her spouse, two cats, one dog, and a plethora of bears, birds, coyotes, and rattlesnakes.

Teresa E. Gallion has lived in Albuquerque, NM since 1987. She completed her undergraduate work at University of Illinois Chicago and her Masters Degree in Psychology from Bowling Green State University in Ohio. She retired from New Mexico state government. She has a chapbook, **Walking Sacred Ground** and a CD, *On the Wings of the Wind*. Her most recent book is **Contemplation in the High Desert** (quatrains inspired by the poetry of Rumi). You may preview her work at http://teresagallion.yolasite.com & www.michaeljohnhallmusic.com.

James M. Gay, Jr. of Placitas, NM, is *Malpaís* Review's staff photographer. His most recent work is in the book **Leaving Cairo, As If It Were A Dream** (Placitas, Malpais Editions, 2012). He will be on the Placitas Art Studio Tour again this year, showing his photography.

Bruce George is a visionary, entrepreneur, speaker, author, panelist, executive producer, writer, poet, consultant, and social activist. Born and raised in New York City, he has written poetry/prose & articles for over 37 years. His work has been published in major magazines, anthologies, and literary publications. He has testimonials from the likes of *Essence Magazine, Emerge Magazine, Class Magazine, Harlem River Press*. Bruce has won multiple poetry & talent contests. He won several awards including "Peabody Award" and a "Miky Award" for "Russell Simmons Presents, Def Poetry Jam (HBO)," an "Upscale Showcase Award," and a "Trail Blazer Award" for his outstanding vision, production, writing and performance. He's Founder/Managing Editor of *The Bandana Republic, an Anthology of Poetry & Prose by Gang Members & Their Affiliates*. As an activist, Bruce has been and currently is associated with major grassroots organizations that foster and uplift people in struggle.

William Georgenes was born in Boston in 1929. He received a BFA from the Mass School of Art and an MFA from Yale University where he studied with James Brooks and Josef Albers. In addition to winning the Blanche Coleman Award, he won first place prizes at the Nantucket Art Association and the Jordan Marsh Contemporary Painting show. He has taught at Harvard University, SUNY Buffalo, the Instituo de Allende, San Miguel de Allende, Mexico and at the DeCordova Museum, Worcester Museum School, and the Boston State Teachers

College. He's had numerous one-man shows including shows at the Contemporaries Gallery, NYC; Our Gallery and Paideia Gallery both in Los Angeles; and in Boston at the Atelier Gallery, Siembab Gallery, and Shore Galleries. His work is in many public and private collections. He lives in Santa Fe and is currently represented by Alex Salazar Gallery, San Diego, CA.

Idris Goodwin is a playwright, poet, essayist, educator, and performer. His genre-defying, hip hop-influenced work for page and stage earned him awards from The National Endowment for the Arts, The Ford Foundation, The Hip Hop Theater Fest and The Illinois Arts Council. His play *How We Got On*, developed at The Eugene O'Neill Theater Center, will premiere at The 2012 Humana Festival of New Plays. This acclaimed hip hop lyricist was praised by *New York Times*, National Public Radio and *The Root Magazine*, who named him in the top 30 performance poets in the world. Idris appeared on HBO's Def Poetry, The Discovery Channel, and most recently, Sesame Street. **These Are The Breaks**, his debut collection of essays, was nominated for a Pushcart Prize. Idris is an adjunct playwriting professor at Northwestern University. Throughout the year this highly sought artist educator gives over fifty performances and lectures at institutions across the country.

Kenneth P. Gurney lives in Albuquerque, NM, with his Dianne. His poetry has been published in many places on the web and in print, but his sentimental favorite is a wall somewhere in New Jersey by a graffiti artist. He edits *Adobe Walls*, an anthology of New Mexico poetry. His latest books are **An Accident Practiced** and **This Is Not Black and White.** To learn more, visit www.kpgurney.me/Poet/Welcome.html.

Dale Harris organizes the annual Sunflower Festival Poets & Writers Picnic at the historic Shaffer Hotel in Mountainair, NM. She edited *Central Avenue*, a monthly poetry journal that sponsored readings in Albuquerque and Santa Fe, from 2002 until it closed in 2007. Her art interests include pottery and making artist books.

Jack Hirschman, born in 1933 in The Bronx, has been a translator and poet in the Haitian struggle for liberation for more than 40 years. He first translated René Depestre's **A Rainbow for the Christian West** from French, and, with Boadiba, translated books of many poets of Haiti and the Haitian diaspora. With Paul Laraque he edited the *Open Gate* anthology of Haitian poetry, also translated with Boadiba. He is the emeritus 4th Poet Laureate of the City of San Francisco (2006-09), the present Poet-in-Residence with The Friends of the San Francisco Public Library and a member of the Revolutionary Poets Brigade.

Bruce Holsapple works as a Speech-Language Pathologist in Magdalena, NM. He's published six books of poetry to date. His most recent is **Vanishing Act** (La Alameda 2010). His poems have appeared in *House Organ, Blue Mesa, First Intensity,* and *Sin Fronteras.* An essay on the verse line in William Carlos Williams' poetry recently appeared in *English Studies in Canada*. He has also recorded poetry under the aegis of Vox Audio for the last eight years, producing CDs by Margaret Randall, Howard McCord, Nathaniel Tarn, Janet Rodney, Joseph Somoza, Álvaro Cardona-Hine, Todd Moore, Gene Frumkin, and Mary Rising Higgins, among others.

George Kalamaras is the author of eleven books of poetry, including **Kingdom of Throat-Stuck Luck** (Elixir Press, 2012), winner of the Elixir Press Poetry contest; **Your Own Ox-Head Mask as Proof** (Ugly Duckling Presse, 2010); **Gold Carp Jack Fruit Mirrors** (The Bitter Oleander Press, 2008); and **The Theory and Function of Mangoes** (Four Way Books, 2000), which won the Four Way Books Intro Series. Two recent collaborations are **Something Beautiful Is Always Wearing the Trees** (Stockport Flats, 2009), George's poems with paintings by Álvaro Cardona-Hine, and **The Recumbent Galaxy** (C & R Press, 2010), co-authored with Cardona-Hine and winner of the C & R Press Open Competition. He is Professor of English at Indiana University-Purdue University Fort Wayne, where he has taught since 1990.

Jon Knudsen edits "The Sunday Poem" at DukeCityFix.com. Over the last three years this series has featured almost 100 Albuquerque area poets and seeks to revive the time when poetry was part of the everyday life of the general reading public. Poetry submissions are always welcome. Email: theditchrider@gmail.com.

Kyle Laws' poems, stories, and essays have appeared in magazines for twenty-five years, with three nominations for a Pushcart Prize. Poetry Motel's Suburban Wilderness Press published a chapbook **Apricot Wounds Straddling the Sky**, and Kings Estate Press put out a collection titled **Tango**. She edited the 2008 poetry volume *From the Garret on Grand: On Miss Lonelyhearts and the Virgin of Guadalupe*, and the 2009 volume *Midnight Train to Dodge*. Lummox Press brought out a full-length poetry collection titled **Wildwood** in 2011.

Wayne Lee's poems have appeared in *Tupelo Press, Slipstream, New Millennium, The Ledge, The California Quarterly, New Mexico Poetry Review, Adobe Walls, The Floating Bridge Anthology* and other journals and anthologies. His collections include **Doggerel & Caterwauls: Poems Inspired by Cats and Dogs** (Red Mountain Press), **Twenty Poems from the Blue House** (co-authored with his wife, Alice Lee, Whistle Lake Press) and the forthcoming **Leap, Float** (Red Mountain Press). He lives in Santa Fe, where he works as an educator and journalist. (wayneleepoet.com)

Jane Lipman's chapbooks, **The Rapture of Tulips** and **White Crow's Secret Life**, published by Pudding House Publications, were finalists for New Mexico Book Awards in Poetry in 2009 and 2010, respectively. Her poems have appeared widely in journals and anthologies.

E. A. "Tony" Mares, Professor Emeritus from the University of New Mexico, is one of the state's most well-known writers. A journalist and historian as well as a poet, his works on Padre Martínez are important contributions to both history and literature. He was a part of the Chicano Literature renaissance centered in Embudo, NM. His latest books of poetry include: **With the Eyes of a Raptor, Astonishing Light (Conversations I Never Had with Patrocinio Barela)** (UNM Press) and *Casi Toda la Musica* (translations of poems by Spanish poet Angel Gonzalez). He lives in Albuquerque.

Steven Martínez is a graduate of UNM, and works closely with the local film industry. Over the years, he's resided in six different states but recently returned home to New Mexico and turned his attention to writing poetry. His work has been published in *The Rag* and the online journal *The New Inquiry*. He resides in Albuquerque, where he's finishing his first chapbook of poetry, **Absence of Epilogue**.

James McGrath of Santa Fe has three collections of poetry with Sunstone Press of Santa Fe: **At the Edgelessness of Light** (2005), **Speaking with Magpies** (2007), **and Dreaming Invisible Voices** (2009). He was former Creative Writing teacher at the Institute of American Indian Arts and presently guides writers at the Ponce De Leon Retirement Center of Santa Fe. James was USIA Arts America poet-artist-in-residence in Yemen, The Kingdom of Saudi Arabia, and The Republic of The Congo in the 1990s.

E. Ethelbert Miller is a major poet who is the author of nine books of poetry, two memoirs and the editor of three anthologies. He has taught at several universities, such as American University, Bennington College, Emory & Henry College, George Mason University, UNLV, and for many years has directed the African-American Resource Center at Howard University, his alma mater. He is currently Board Chairman of the Institute for Policy Studies, a progressive think tank located in Washington, D.C., Editor of *Poet Lore* magazine and Founder/Director of the Ascension Poetry Series, one of the oldest in the Washington, D.C. area. He is former Chairperson of the Washington, D.C. Humanities Council. His latest book, a second memoir, is **The 5th Inning** (2009).

Jill A. Oglesby was born and raised in Albuquerque, New Mexico. She now lives in Los Lunas with her tuxedo cat, Binks, and her labrador, Buíochas. She has been published in *Southwestern Women, New Voices; Friends Journal (Philadelphia); Artistica; the Blue Mesa Review; The Fixed and Free Anthology; The Rag;* and *Adobe Walls #2*.

Bill O'Neill grew up in rural Central Ohio, graduated from Cornell University, and currently is in his second term as State Representative in the NM Legislature. Bill's poetry has appeared in the *New York Quarterly, Rolling Stock,* and more recently in the *Santa Fe Literary Review* and *New Mexico Poetry Review*. Bill works as the Development Director for a program run through the NM Conference of Churches that mentors high-risk juvenile offenders upon their release from CYFD custody.

Holly Prado has been one of the most well-known poets in Los Angeles for the last 35 years. She has published ten books of poetry and prose and is one of the founders of Cahuenga Press. She has reviewed poetry and fiction for the *Los Angeles Times,* and her own work has appeared in more than 100 periodicals, including *The Paris Review, Kenyon Review, Exquisite Corpse, American Poetry Review, Colorado Review, Indiana Review* and in more than a dozen anthologies. She has taught in the Poetry-in-the-Schools program as well as at USC, Beyond Baroque Foundation, and the LA Woman's Building. Her work has been honored by the LA Cultural Affairs Department, and in 2000 she was awarded First Prize in the *Fin du Millenium* competition sponsored by the Los Angeles Poetry Festival. Her latest book, **Monkey Journal**, was published in 2009 by Tebot Bach Press. Álvaro Cardona-Hine was one of her mentors when he lived in LA.

Margaret Randall, though born in New York City, grew up in Albuquerque, and claims the mountains and deserts in her work. In the 1960s, she co-founded and edited *El Corno Emplumado / The Plumed Horn,* a seminal bilingual literary journal of the era. She lived in Latin America (Mexico, Cuba, Nicaragua) for a quarter century. She has published more than 100 books of poetry and prose, most recently: **To Change the World (My Years in Cuba),** (a prose memoir); **Stones Witness** and **Their Backs to the Sea** (both poetry); **My Town** (poetry, prose and photographs); and **Ruins** (poetry, UNM Press).

Don Russ is the author of **Dream Driving** (Kennesaw State University Press, 2007) and the chapbook **Adam's Nap** (Billy Goat Press, 2005). He publishes regularly and widely in literary magazines.

Sonia Sánchez is the author of more than 20 books of poetry, seven plays, several children's books and many essays. She attended Hunter College and NYU, where she studied with poet Louise Bogan. She has taught at eight different universities and read her work on some 500 campuses and around the world. She was an activist in the Black Arts Movement, a member of CORE, and knew Malcolm X. She has won many awards including an NEA Fellowship, the PEN Writing Award, American Book Award, the Robert Creeley Award, Harper Lee Award, and a Pew Fellowship. She is Poet Laureate of Philadelphia and is known for experimenting with music, haiku and tanka. She is not only a major poet but also a mother and grandmother. Her latest book is **Morning Haiku** (Beacon Press, 2010).

Stephen Sargent - An experienced administrator and organizer, Stephen received his PhD from Texas A&M University in 2009, where he studied public administration, and was the North Texas Field Director for a U.S. Senate Campaign. He has been the member of three National Poetry Slam teams: the 2005 Fort Worth Slam Team which ranked 3rd the nation, the 2006 Fort Worth Slam Team Team which reached the semifinals and the 2007 Bryan Slam Team. In 2006 he released his first spoken word album *"GOD Speaks."*

Andrea J. Serrano, native of Albuquerque, NM, has been writing and performing poetry since 1994. Andrea has been published in various publications including *Cantos al Sexto Sol: An Anthology of Aztlanahuac Writings* (Rodriguez/Gonzales). Andrea is the youngest of six daughters and credits her family, her ties to land, language and culture and the experience of growing up Chicana in Albuquerque with influencing her writing. Andrea is a member of the band *Cultura Fuerte*, and is the creator and host of Speak, Poet: *Voz, Palabra y Sonido*, a monthly poetry venue.

Jonathan Slator has been published in several mountaineering magazines including, *Climbing, High Tor,* and *Mountain.* Many years ago Birmingham University Press, UK, published his poetry. He has spent the majority of his working life in the film business in a range of roles including producer, assistant director, actor, stunt driver, and, lately, as location scout and manager. He has worked on movie projects on all continents except Antarctica. He is the Founding Director of the Taos Mountain Film Festival. (js@mountainfilm.net)

Sherod Smallman, born and raised in North Philly, began a interest in poetry at a very young age. Inspired by his mother, who is also a poet, Sherod wrote his first poem at age 6 but didn't take it seriously until he was 19, when he saw the Twin Poets at a college poetry show. Since that moment, he has a love for the spoken word. His love for poetry grew deeper when he found out about the Slam competition, which combined two of his loves: spoken word and competition. He has won and placed in several slams and competed in the 2007 National Poetry Slam on team Delawhere. But the proudest moment in his poetry career was Oct. 27, 2007, the day The Fuze, the First Poetry Slam Inc Certified Venue in Philly, was born. Sherod is founder of The Fuze and has been a slam master for 3 years. The Fuze has sent 2 teams and 4 individual poets to multiple competitions nationwide.

Suzi Q. Smith lives with her brilliant daughter in Denver. Her work has appeared in a number of literary magazines and anthologies, and she is currently among the highest ranked slam poets in the nation. She travels the nation performing and teaching poetry and music.

Marilyn Stablein's collages, assemblages, and award-winning artist books are exhibited in museums, libraries, galleries, and arts centers. In addition to creating the cover collages for this issue, her art is featured in *Santa Fe Review, Kyoto Journal, Rattle Magazine, Raven Chronicles* and at galleries at the University of California, University of Nebraska, Towson University, and the Delaware Center for Contemporary Art. She is also author of eleven books including **Splitting Hard Ground** which won the New Mexico Book Award and the National Federation of Press Women's book award. She teaches classes in memoir writing and poetry and co-owns with her husband Acequia Booksellers, a fine used bookstore in Albuquerque's North Valley and online at *acequiabooksellers.com.*

Judith Toler has been an editor, an English professor, and a faculty union organizer. Currently retired, she now divides her time between making art and writing poetry. Her poems have won a New Mexico Discovery Award as well as awards from *Passager* and *the Santa Fe Reporter*. Most recently her work has appeared in *Adobe Walls, Cha: An Asian Literary Journal, Lilliput, New Mexico Poetry Review,* and *Santa Fe Poetry Broadside.*

John Tritica – Albuquerque poet John Tritica, a teacher by profession, studied at UCSD, UNM, Miami University, and Lund University in Sweden, where he knew the Swedish poet Niklas Törnlund. He has translated Törnlund's poetry in a volume called **All Things Measure Time**. He has also published his own poetry widely in many journals and in books including **How Rain Records Its Alphabet** and **Sound Remains**.

Dr. Charles Trumbull is retired from editing and publishing positions at the U.S. National Academy of Sciences, Radio Free Europe/ Radio Liberty, and Encyclopædia Britannica. A past president of the Haiku Society of America, since 2006 he has been editor of the journal *Modern Haiku*, now based in Santa Fe. His haiku have been published and anthologized widely for twenty years and his haiku chapbook, **Between the Chimes**, was published in 2011. Recently his longer poems have appeared in *Adobe Walls, New Mexico Poetry Review,* and *Malpaís Review.*

María Vázquez Valdéz is an up-and-coming Mexican poet from Zacatecas, currently living in Mexico City. Among her books are: *Estancias* (2004), a collection of cultural essays; *Rayuela de museos* (2005), a large volume about the world's most important art museums, text and photos by the author; and *Caldero* (1999) and *Estaciones del albatros* (2008), both poetry books. She is editor-in-chief of the important arts magazine *Arcilla roja (Red Clay),* has translated the poems of others, works as a free-lance editor and photographer, and is known for organizing exciting poetry events.

Idea Vilariño (1920-2009) was one of Uruguay's most well known poets and essayists, famous for her minimal style of "naked words" (as one critic called it) that left the reader alone with few words but lots of meaning, provoking thought. She published some 15 books of poetry and anthologies between 1945 and 2006, and was also a teacher. Her most famous work, published and republished in various editions over the years is *Poemas del Amor* **(Love Poems)**. It is generally accepted that these poems are related to her tempestuous relationship to the even more famous Uruguayan novelist & short story writer, Juan Carlos Onetti, which never resulted in a permanent arrangement. Vilariño was a member of Uruguay's "Generation of 1945," which included many of the nation's major writers of the 20th Century. She co-founded two important literary journals, composed music, and translated the works of

William Henry Hudson and Shakespeare into Spanish, the latter resulting in stage productions. Her complete works were published in 2002.

Linda Whittenberg went from pastoring to poetry when she retired from Unitarian Universalist ministry in 2000. Her work has been widely published in journals and anthologies. She has published **Dying Can Wait** (Pudding House Publications) and **Tender Harvest**, finalist for the New Mexico Book Award. **Somewhere in Ireland**, a collection of Irish-inspired poems, has just been released. She makes her home in Santa Fe with her husband Robert Wilber and their animal companions—a mule, a goat, and two cattle dogs. For more, visit www.lindawhittenberg.com

Tanaya Winder is from Southern Ute and Duckwater Shoshone Nations. She is a winner of A Room Of Her Own Foundation's Spring 2010 Orlando poetry prize. Tanaya's work has appeared or is forthcoming in *Cutthroat, Adobe Walls, Superstition Review, Kweli, and Drunkenboat* among others. She is currently pursuing an MFA at the UNM.

Richard Wolfson began writing after the death of his wife JoAnn, a poet, in 2004. Many of these poems come from dreams and shamanic journeys. He currently lives in Albuquerque with his second wife Vicki Bolen, an artist who collaborates with him on books, cards, and prints.

Vox Audio

Compact Disks of Contemporary Poetry

Howard McCord Reads at the Anasazi Fields Winery
        Recorded in Placitas, NM October 30, 2011

Howard McCord Reads
        Recorded in Magdalena, NM October 27, 2011

Amalio Madueño and Álvaro Cardona-Hine Read
        at the Anasazi Fields Winery
        Recorded in Placitas, NM September 11, 2011

Mei-Mei Berssenbrugge and Jonathan Skinner Read at Acequia Booksellers
        Recorded in Albuquerque, NM January 23, 2011

John Tritica Reads "Fire in the New Year" and "Resonant Vocation"
        Recorded in Magdalena, NM December 21, 2010

Suzanne Lummis and Margaret Randall Read at the Anasazi Fields Winery
        Recorded in Placitas, NM September 12, 2010

Carol Moldaw Reads at Acequia Booksellers
        Recorded in Albuquerque, NM August 29, 2010

Stanley Noyes Reads
        Recorded in Santa Fe, NM August 26, 2010

George Kalamaras and Álvaro Cardona-Hine Read at Acequia Booksellers
        Recorded in Albuquerque, NM July 18, 2010

Lawrence Welsh Reads
        Recorded in Magdalena, NM May 25, 2010

A Memorial Reading for Todd Moore
        Recorded at the Harwood Art Center in Albuquerque, NM
        May 22, 2010

Marilyn Stablein Reads at Acequia Booksellers
        Recorded in Albuquerque, NM April 25, 2010

V.B. Price Reads at Acequia Booksellers
        Recorded in Albuquerque, NM March 14, 2010

Amy Beeder and Stefi Weisburd Read at Acequia Booksellers
        Recorded in Albuquerque, NM January 17, 2010

Donald Levering and Janine Pommy-Vega Read at the Anasazi Fields Winery
Recorded in Placitas, NM January 10, 2010

Anne Valley-Fox Reads at Acequia Booksellers
Recorded in Albuquerque, NM November 29, 2009

Keith Wilson Reads from Lion's Gate Volume One
Recorded in Santa Fe, NM 1990

Keith Wilson Reads from Lion's Gate Volume Two
Recorded in Santa Fe, NM 1990

John Clarke and Charles Keil in Performance
Recorded in Buffalo, NY May 20, 1984 and March 13,1985

Donald Guravich and Joanne Kyger Read at the Anasazi Fields Winery
Recorded in Placitas, NM September 13, 2009

Todd Moore and Lawrence Welsh Read at Acequia Booksellers
Recorded in Albuquerque, NM July 12, 2009

Ann McGinnis, Anne MacNaughton and Peter Rabbit Read at the Anasazi
Fields Winery, Recorded in Placitas, NM March 15, 2009

Joseph Somoza Reads
Recorded in Las Cruces, NM February 9, 2009

Wayne Crawford Reads
Recorded in Las Cruces, NM February 9, 2009

Michael Boughn Reads from Cosmographia
Recorded in Toronto, ON January 2009

Nathaniel Tarn Reads
Recorded in Magdalena, NM October 5, 2008

Janet Rodney Reads
Recorded in Magdalena, NM October 5, 2008

John Tritica Reads at Acequia Booksellers
Recorded in Albuquerque, NM September 28, 2008

Joan Logghe Reads
Recorded in Albuquerque, NM September 14, 2008

Nathaniel Tarn Reads at Acequia Booksellers
in Albuquerque, NM September 7, 2008

David Empfield Reads from Love In The KGB
Recorded in St. Paul, MN August 2008

Lee Sharkey Reads from A Darker, Sweeter String
Recorded in Vienna, ME June 16, 2008

Mera Wolf and Todd Moore Read at Acequia Booksellers
in Albuquerque, NM February 24, 2008

Margaret Randall Reads
Recorded in Albuquerque, NM February 21, 2008

John Macker Reads at Acequia Booksellers
in Albuquerque, NM January 13, 2008

Albert Huffstickler – 'Huff' – Reads
Recorded in Austin, TX 1987-9 and Bisbee, AZ 1991

David Benedetti Reads
Recorded in Albuquerque, NM December 20, 2007

Gary Brower Reads
Recorded in Magdalena, NM November 17, 2007

Michael Rothenberg and David Meltzer Read at the Outpost
in Albuquerque, NM October 12, 2007

Jeffrey Lee and David Abel Read at Acequia Booksellers
in Albuquerque, NM June 3, 2007

Burt Hatlen: New Poems
Recorded in Bangor and Orono, ME June 2006-7

Remembering Gene: A Memorial Reading of His Poetry
Recorded in Albuquerque, NM March 30, 2007

Tribute To Lorca: The Duende Poetry Series at the Anasazi Fields Winery,
including Cirrelda and Jeff Bryan, Joan Logghe, Leo
Romero, and Gary Brower, Placitas, NM, January 21, 2007,

Bobby Byrd and Joe Hayes at the Outpost
in Albuquerque, NM November 11, 2006

Mary Rising Higgins, George Kalamaras, Mary Ann Cain and Gene
Frumkin Read at the Harwood Art Center
in Albuquerque, NM July 19, 2006

Jim Bishop Reads
Recorded in Bangor, ME June 2006

Larry Goodell Live! Reading at the Anasazi Fields Winery
in Placitas, NM June 11, 2006

Chico Martin Reads
Recorded in Magdalena, NM March 2, 2006

Bill Sylvester Reads
Recorded in Buffalo, NY February 2006

Todd Moore Reads
>   Recorded in Magdalena, NM February 24, 2006

Craig Dworkin and Mary Rising Higgins Read
>   Recorded in Albuquerque, NM February 11, 2006

Duende and Friends: A Poetry Reading at the Anasazi Fields Winery
>   Recorded in Placitas, NM January 22, 2006

John Tritica Reads
>   Recorded in Magdalena, NM December 28, 2005

Burt Hatlen Reads
>   Recorded in Bangor, ME June 27, 2005

Dana Wilde Reads
>   Recorded in Troy, ME June 28, 2005

Joseph Somoza Reads at the Anasazi Fields Winery
>   in Placitas, NM June 11, 2005

Bruce Holsapple Reads from Vanishing Act
>   Recorded in Magdalena, NM June 2005

Mary Rising Higgins Reads
>   Recorded in Magdalena, NM March 5, 2005

Gene Frumkin Reads
>   Recorded in Magdalena, NM March 5, 2005

Bruce Holsapple Reads from Skull of Caves
>   Recorded in Magdalena, NM December 2004

David Empfield Reads from The Horse Opera and Cold Moons
>   Recorded in Magdalena, NM January 2002

Timothy Wright Reads The Dust Of Europe
>   Recorded in East Machias, ME January 1980

Vox Audio

P.O. Box 594 - Magdalena, NM - 87825

available at http://voxaudio.outlawpoetry.com

THE DUENDE POETRY SERIES
OF PLACITAS, NEW MEXICO

**invites you to attend our readings four times per year
(March, June, September & one floating date)
always at 3pm on a Sunday at
Anasazi Fields Winery, Placitas, New Mexico.**

current schedule at www.anasazifieldswinery.com/events

Since 2004, some of our past readers include:

Janine Pommy-Vega with J'Zaam	Bruce Holsapple
Wayne Crawford	Mark Weber
Karen McKinnon	John Orne Green
Dick Thomas	Jason L. Yurcic
Lisa Gill	Art Goodtimes
Dale Harris	Mitch Rayes
Donald Levering	Anne McNaughton
Margaret Randall	Hakim Bellamy
E.A. "Tony" Mares	Peter Rabbit
Todd Moore	J.B. Bryan
Gene Frumkin	Joanne Kyger
Bobby Byrd	Larry Goodell
Levi Romero	Donald Gurevich
Sawnie Morris	Gary L. Brower
Maria Leyba	John Macker
Renny Golden	Jim Fish
Simon Ortiz with	Cirrelda Snyder-Bryan
Sara Marie & Rainy Dawn Ortiz	Luci Tapahonso
Michelle Holland	Mary Oishi
Suzanne Lummis	Joan Logghe
John Tritica	Anne Valley Fox
Marilyn Stablein	Joy Harjo (with her band)
Mary McGinnis	Stefan Hyner
Don McIver	Maisha Baton
Heloise Wilson	Jim Koller
Leo Romero	Enrique LaMadrid
Doris Fields	Albino Carrillo
Joe Somoza	Bill Pearlman
Gary Mex Glazner	Amalio Madueño
Richard Vargas	Álvaro Cardona-Hine
Howard McCord	Carol Moscrip
Rich Boucher	Debbie Coy

Credits

POEMS & ESSAYS

Sonia Sánchez's three haikus are all from her latest book, **Morning Haiku**, copyright 2009 by Sonia Sánchez; reprinted by permission of Beacon Press, Boston.

Álvaro Cardona-Hine's "Spring," "Summer," "Autumn," "Winter" haiku from **The Gathering Wave** (Denver, Alan Swallow, Publisher, 1961). "Words Again," "Hermitage," "Putting Your Shadow On Backwards" from **A Garden Of Sound** (Redmond, Wa., Pemmican Press, 1996). "Listen Galaxea" from **Words on Paper,** (Los Angeles, Red Hill Press, 1974). Permission to use "Goya," "Segovia," and "Mussorgsky Dreams" from **The Curvature of the Earth** (Albuquerque, University of New Mexico Press, 2007) was given by the author.

Gene Frumkin's "Escalator" and "Narrative of Conscience" are from **Freud By Other Means.** "Back Seat Dodge '38, 1964," "Blue Horse," "Crowded Air," "In Memoriam 9/11," "That Civil War in Spain," are from **Meditations in Crowded Air**, edited by David Abel, forthcoming from Chax Press.

Idea Vilariño's poems were translated by Gary L. Brower from *Orientales: Uruguay a traves de su poesia* (Amir Hamed, Ed.; Montevideo, Casa Editorial HUM, 2010).

Andrea Serrano's "Lament" is published in an anthology *¡Ban This! The BSP Anthology of Xican@ Literature* published by Broken Sword Press.

Charles Trumbull's "Gleaners: Romania, 1990" was previously published in Romanian, translated by Richard Wiest, in *Alianta Civica* (Bucharest) Nr. 3 (serie noua) 27 xi-4 xii 1991, pag. 16.

María Vázquez Valdéz's poem "Flight" is unpublished even in Spanish; "Coagulated Blood" is from *Caldero* (Ediciones Alforja, Mexico, 1999); "One" is previously unpublished; all translations by Margaret Randall.

Harvena Richter's poems "Meeting," "The Island," "Burrs," "Corn Mother" from **The Innocent Island.** "IV The Seed," "VII Geode," "XII Twinned Crystals," "XVI Flaw," "XXII Crystal as Temple" are from **Frozen Light: The Crystal Poems.** Permission to use Harvena Richter poems is from David R. Johnson who is in charge of her estate.

PHOTOS & ART

Mitch Rayes receives belated credit for his photo of Bob Swearingen in the Winter issue.

Marilyn Stablein is thanked for the exciting collages on our covers.

William Georgenes is thanked for his gracious cooperation in providing images of his assemblage sculptures.

Title page photo is by James M. Gay, Jr.

"Adrienne Rich at Ghost Ranch, New Mexico, 1990s" photo by Margaret Randall. "Audre Lorde, Meridel LeSueur, and Adrienne Rich, 1980" photo credit: K.Kendall/Flickr.

Hakim Bellamy as Poet Laureate, photo by Margaret Randall.

Photo of Álvaro Cardona-Hine and George Kalamaras is by Bruce Holsapple, July 2010.

Gene Frumkin photo (p. 126) taken about 2000 at a National Poetry Foundation conference in Orono, Maine, is by Bruce Holsapple. Photo of Gene Frumkin, fall 1996, (p. 136) is by Sharon Matthews DiMaria.

John Tritica photo (p. 153) is by Margaret Randall.

Photo of the *Librotraficante* event is courtesy of Hakim Bellamy.

Photo of María Vázquez Valdéz is by Margaret Randall.

Richter family photo was done by Knopf photographer Elliot Erwitt. It was taken at the same time he did the photo for the release of **The Town** in 1950. **The Town**, of course, is the book for which Conrad Richter received the Pulitzer Prize. Permission to use photos is from David R. Johnson who is in charge of Harvena's estate. Harvena Richter, 2008, photo is by Jon Knudsen.

Submission Guidelines

Malpaís **Review** is a 6"x9" hardcopy publication between 120 and 220 pages each issue. Reading Periods: for Spring issue: Oct, Nov, Dec; for Summer issue: Jan, Feb, Mar; for Autumn issue: Apr, May, Jun; for Winter issue: Jul, Aug, Sep.

Poems: *Malpaís* **Review** seeks original poems, previously unpublished in North America, written in English. Any topic, but please no hate-inciting or pornographic work. Submit 1 to 5 poems, no limit on length, but once you hit 10 pages call the submission done (unless the submission is a single poem that is longer than 10 pages). One submission per reading period. Notification of acceptance will take place within 1 month of the closing of a reading period. If your work is accepted into an issue, please let one issue go by before you submit again. In other words, we will publish your work a maximum of twice a year in an effort to keep the voices fresh. No simultaneous submissions. The editor reserves the right to edit and cannot be held liable for the occasional typo or formatting error.

Essay: Topics: poetic criticism, history, theory, a specific poet or poem. Essays should be original and previously unpublished in North

America. Length may be up to 5,000 words.

Translations: Translations of both poems and essays will be considered. Required: permission of the original poet is required along with a copy of the poem in its original language (assumes poet is living and/or copyrights are still in force). We intend to publish both the original poem and the translation if space permits.

Featured Poets: Will be invited by the editorial staff for each issue.

Artwork: 1 to 3 digital images should be saved as JPG (JPEG), at a resolution of 300 dpi. Make sure you set your email to attach the "actual" image instead of allowing the email program to reduce the image size. Set images to CYMK. If the image is selected for showing in the interior of the issue, it will be converted to grayscale.

How/Where: Electronic submissions are preferred. Please send your poems in the body of an email. Due to the risk of viruses, we will discard, without reading, all emails with attachments. If your poems have unusual formatting, note it, and we will ask for a file attachment (such as pdf, doc, or rtf file) if the work is accepted.

In the subject line of the email, please place the words POETRY or ESSAY, a dash, then your name. Example: poetry-JQ Public. Email ONLY to **poetry@Malpaísreview.com.**

If you do not have access to email, please send hardcopy to: *Malpaís* **Review**, po box 339, Placitas, NM 87043. Include a SAS Envelope or Postcard for response. Submissions without SAS Envelope or Postcard will be discarded without reading them.

Submit ARTWORK in a separate email from poems or essays. Artwork may only be submitted via email, to **art@Malpaísreview.com**.

Please include a short, third-person **biography** with your submission.

Rights: *Malpaís* **Review** seeks first North American Rights of your work to appear in our hardcopy publication, and reserves the right to use your work in a future "best of" issue. Rights revert to author/artist upon publication.

Made in the USA
Charleston, SC
20 May 2012